CHEW ON IT   LOVE-HANDLES

PUT ON SOCKS

BEAUTIFUL MEMORIES

LEND A HAND

HIGHS AND LOWS

MY NEIGHBOR ASKED   EAR HAIR

COOL PEOPLE

MY LIFE

DING HANDS

LAUGHING

OF

FREESTYLE

WHAT YALL DOING IN HERE?

FOCUS

LISTS.

HOLDING HANDS...WITH A STRANGER

BOOTYQUAKES

VOLUME 1

HUG MORE OFTEN

THE EXTRA MILE

DERRICK SIER

NDS

KIDS SLEEP

My Life of Lists. Volume 1
By Derrick D. Sier

Copyright © 2018 by Derrick D. Sier.
All rights reserved.

Published by Derrick Sier & OMOS Team Building.
PO BOX 721395 Oklahoma City, Oklahoma 73172
405.412.0473

International Standard Book Number: 978-1727847246
Printed in the United States of America

Cover design and formatting by
Kristen McGregor - Astrea Design.

Group Edit by Derrick Sier, Tequia Sier,
Mirjana Terzic

MY LIFE

OF

LISTS.

DERRICK SIER

TABLE OF CONTENTS

INTRODUCTION

This project was something I originally started doing for fun. I had no intention of it becoming something of this magnitude. But just like anything worth something, it kind of took on a life of its own. But in order to effectively introduce you to the concept, I have to tell you how "My Life of Lists" came about.

One of the things I love about being an entrepreneur is the flexibility of my schedule. And one of the first things I added to my schedule upon becoming an entrepreneur was picking my kids up from school. While my being able to pick up my kids after school benefited our family in several ways, the most rewarding benefit, and the thing I had come to love the most was the one thing I never even considered beforehand: the conversation. That's right. Simply talking with my kids. No agenda. Just kid talk. Car talk. No mom. Just a dad with his ten year old daughter (yikes!) and nine year old son talking about school and life. It was absolutely eye-opening. Picking my kids up right after school meant I was able to access their entire day while it was fresh on their brains. Right after the bell would ring, they'd say so-long to friends, hop into my car and guess who would get their day?! ME! And after a long day of talking to adults about grown up things, picking my kids up from school and hearing about their day was a treat. In fact, I often found it refreshing to get a child's perspective on life after dealing with my own.

As a part of our after-school conversation, I would ask two questions: What was something you learned today? What was something cool that happened today?

Initially, my daughter, being the mature 5th grader she was, would rarely share something voluntarily. I'd have to pry it out of her. Well, let me correct that. I think her "maturing" was part of the reason she wouldn't share. The other part was her being concerned that her cool-o-meter wouldn't match up with mine. Based on previous conversations, she was worried that I would think her cool stories were lame. She was right, I did. I thought they were super lame, in fact. I mean, come on. Parents, help me out. How many times have you listened to your children's drama stories about fifth grade and thought to yourself, "Baby, within the grand scheme of life, your pony tail coming down during the assembly is such a small thing." Am I right?! I know I'm right. But that wasn't the point. Because of my responses, she didn't feel safe to share. That was my fault. She would talk about something she thought was amazing or huge in her life and I'd instantly become critical, tell her how un-cool it was or under-respond to something she thought was super-response worthy. So, now that I am picking her up from school and I am inviting her to share again, she was resistant. Understandably so. If I was her, I would be hesitant to share with me as well. That said, getting her to share, initially, was difficult. Eventually, my wife corrected me. I corrected my responses. And when I did, my daughter began to open up and share even the smallest of details. And I thought that was awesome! I sincerely did. The after-school conversations between my daughter and I opened my heart to a realm of the father-daughter relationship I had been totally missing out on. And now that the door has been opened, it stays wide open and we talk about everything. I hope it never closes.

My son, on the other hand, didn't have any qualms about sharing. Granted, since I thought his stories were a bit more entertaining, mainly because he was talking about stuff I was naturally more interested in, he didn't initially have to press through my unreceptive responses. This clear path to sharing allowed my son to share in what appeared to be a random order. If someone asked me about my day, I would start at the beginning and work forward toward the present moment. But this guy would share as the thoughts came to his memory. Then something remarkable happened. The more he would begin to share, the more my daughter began to share. It was as if they were tag-teaming the day. He would start a story and she would fill in the blanks. Or maybe it was more like a relay and they both were running multiple legs. He would run with the story, hand it off to her, she would hand it back, then he would hand it back to her to bring it home with the punch line.

I loved it! I loved it so much. By giving my kids permission to share, then watching them recall everything they learned and all of the cool experiences they encountered individually and together throughout the day, I was gaining access to a part of them that would have otherwise remained untapped. The more they shared, the more I would ask. The more I asked, the more it forced them to be more creative in their explanation. The creativity added color to their stories and caused them to be a bit more observant because they knew, in addition to the obvious components to the story, I was going to ask them about the details as well. It was such a joy. It was inspiring, in fact. So, I decided to start experiencing for myself what I made available to my children: the ability to observe the world around me, reflect in no particular order and intentionally retain and appreciate all of the cool things I learn and experience throughout my day. Now, at the end of the day or the end of any particular moment, I always give myself permission and time to reflect. This project is the result of those thoughts.

When I first started doing this, I wanted to catch moments around me no one else would even bother to notice. OR moments everyone would notice, but probably wouldn't say out loud. OR moments everyone would notice, say out loud and everyone would enjoy...together! As I began to pay more attention to these moments, I would share them with people around me. In general conversation, I would mention a meeting or a car ride or someone I noticed at a stop light or a conversation my kids were having in the back seat or people at church doing funny/silly things or two birds in a tree or something I saw in a store. Anything. The smallest of things. The responses I would receive from sharing were often met with laughs and even more so, provoked further conversation. And since I see the world through humor and hugs, my perception will always have a humorous and personal slant. That said, I expected a positive response, but the responses I was getting were almost surreal.

My friend, Taylor, mentioned sharing my thoughts on

social media in a more intentional format. I initially thought it would be one of those things you'd have to share in person. You know, those stories you need to hear and see the story teller in order for it to carry the full weight of delivery? I thought it would be like that. But when I went from sharing in person to sharing on social media, that's when the list concept went from being a personal goal to something I was able to use to positively impact the people in the small world around me. Now, I'm no celebrity by any means. I don't claim to be anyone significant, but I get around my small city. I'm very social. Half of meeting people and building community is genuinely being nice, genuinely being interested in people and supporting community efforts. The other half is actually getting out, being active where the people are and being involved in what they are doing. That is something I hold near to my heart and I try to live those three concepts in every area of my life. That said, that attitude and perspective has allowed me to meet quite a few people in my city and those people … know people. It's through that avenue I've built relationships.

I would be in a restaurant and people would come up to me and mention my posts. I have been waved down in traffic. School administrators have taken my approach and implemented it into their end-of-the-day classroom discussions. Marriage counselors have recommended it to their couples. I've gotten stand-up comedy gigs and several speaking opportunities based on them. It had gotten bigger than I ever could have imagined.

The truth is, I hadn't done anything special. People notice and interact with the environment around them all of the time. But what I did was notice the world through my silly little lens. And guess what?! You have a lens too. You know, that tilt or skew that makes you…you. For me, I like small gestures of affection like the husband who brushes the cracker crumbs from the front of his wife's shirt just to graze her breast. I like catching people digging in their noses at stop lights. I like seeing people trip and then watching them look around to see who saw them. I like catching sneaky little kids doing stuff I enjoy doing as an adult, like unscrewing the parmesan cheese tops at pizza buffets. I like watching professional golfers hit a fat shot, then use their hats to cover the curse words coming out of their mouths. I like catching people drop food on the floor, pick it up and eat it. I like breaking cultural norms, then observing people's response to them. I like seeing dads completely crush their kids in sports and games. I like seeing awkward handshakes and unwanted hugs.

Does this make me strange? Maybe. But I don't think I'm the only one. I think there are people out there like me who take joy in experiencing the little joys of life serving as hidden gems for those who take the extra time to laugh a bit louder, hug a little tighter, stare a bit longer and love a tad deeper.

So, this book is for the people who bend down to smell the roses and notice the humping worms; for the people who count the number of "umms" during their co-workers' presentation; who notice the people who bring food to the potluck but never wash their hands before leaving the restroom; whose heart beats fast when watching lovers hold hands; who notice the boom mic in B-movies; who notice the single standing tree in the pasture; who seek to make the neglected feel included; who let their daughter play with toy cars without wiping the dirt from her face and let their little boy play with baby dolls and a kitchen set. For all of those people, I hope you enjoy "My Life of Lists" and like my children, give yourself permission to reflect, dream, absorb, interact with, list without order and perceive the world around you through YOUR lens – one of the single most important freedoms any individual can possess.

I'll say it again: take joy in experiencing the little joys of life. They serve as gems for those who take the extra time to find them. How do you find them? Laugh loudly. Hug tightly. Stare longer. Love deeper. And write on your heart a list of everything that brings you joy…from now until eternity.

DEDICATION:

TO MY TEN SQUAD.

TO MY FATHER.

The brightest social butterfly in the garden of life.

ACKNOWLEDGMENTS

This book never happens without Taylor Doe. Without his vision and stubborn encouragement, this concept doesn't even exist. Without our late-night work seshes, 1:00 am Whataburger runs, Thursday night visits to Vast, James Stuart breakfasts, Grandy's and Chic-Fil-A power lunches, road trip think tanks, pop-up community events, hands & feet conversations.... without our tear-filled prayers for justice and reconciliation, marriage talks, 3:00 am texts, breakout whiteboard brain dumps... without our transparent and sincere desire to use relationship as an avenue to bring about change...without seeing the world the way we do together.... this book doesn't happen.

I love you brother. Our conversations are woven throughout this book.

WAIT...

I've always wondered how I would read a book if someone told me the end at the beginning. Instead of having to read the book to get the information, how would I read the book knowing the exact angle the author would take and the exact points the author would make? In the same manner, how would I live life differently given the opportunity to stand at the end looking back towards the beginning? How would I enter an argument knowing the outcome of every scenario? I've thought about this with marriage, work, friends, religion....the whole gamut. You have too.

You have stood on the back end of a situation and said, "Man, I wish I would have done that differently." And having locked in what you believed would be the better alternative, you made that statement thinking a different decision would have brought about your desired end. Or maybe the thought wasn't created because of dissatisfaction, but more out of curiosity. "It's not that I'm displeased with [*insert whatever situation in which you've become complacent*], but I just wonder what would have happened if [*insert different scenario than the one you chose*]." I've been there. I do it still. What I've found is that either that reflection process causes us to be more prepared for the next moment or it causes us to resent the current situation and be frozen and ill-shaped by regret and dissatisfaction.

For those of you who look at these moments as learning opportunities, you will grow and move on to dominate the next crucial decision. I applaud you for not getting stuck. It's easy to get stuck, complacent and discouraged in those moments. Instead, you moved forward. You are moving forward. It's not an aimless movement, but you're moving toward perfecting your decision-making process and eliminating the need for regret. And not that it will be perfect, but the process through which you approach those moments will be consistent and always in the state of being perfected. My wife and I have always been great roommates. We divide and conquer our to-do list. We communicate and complete tasks well. We have always covered the other regarding chores, duties and responsibilities. We are both clean and orderly. Because of our personalities, those things came natural to us. Not so much when it came to being husband and wife. Over time, we have had to intentionally and consistently work on being great spouses. We have stood on the back end of some decisions and thought some of the same thoughts listed above. But instead of getting caught up in offense, disappointment, hopelessness and regret, we used those reflections as an opportunity to shape our future decisions. We haven't arrived at perfection, probably never will, but we will never stop pursuing it and are determined to arrive there....together. For you, if you think the same way about your life and your goals and your relationships; if you identify with the above paragraph, this book will be confirmation, encouragement and a boost in what you're already doing.

For those of you who find yourself stuck often, I hope this book provides you with some escape options to consider. Not escaping one situation just to become stuck in another, but to become a professional escape artist and consistently move towards happiness and fulfillment; towards being able to identify and elude potential potholes and snares. Keep in mind, regret anchors you to the past, disappointment misshapes your expectations and complacently prevents you from reaching your full potential. When you loose the grip of those things on your life, you will eventually shake free and run towards whatever fulfills you the most. This goes for every area of your life and any situation that may arise. For you, this book will give you examples of how the mundane can entertain; how to turn nope into hope; how to speak and think life into every situation. You'll see how the simplest of things can become simply marvelous in the light of a positive and optimistic perspective. You *can* control how you interact with the world around you.

So, it's the beginning of the book. Before you flip another

page, I want you to know the flow of the book, where we are going and how it will end. Use this information to reflect on your life during the book, NOT AT THE END! Don't wait until the end to apply these concepts to your life. Apply as you go. Every sentence. If you don't, you're not reading it right. And I will know…and karate chop your soul from wherever I am in the world. Punishment is the most passive threat that I can muster. So, here we go.

This book has 30 social media posts with comments from some of my friends and followers; many of which will be acknowledged. All 30 posts were collected over the span of a year. Each post will be dated. Most of these posts will be in the form of lists. I will pick one item or topic from that list and expound on the life lesson I learned from looking at that one item differently and a bit longer than the others. My reflection process will be divided into three parts: **1) the story behind the item, 2) the obvious observation and 3) the deeper lesson I learned once I dissected it a bit more.** Yes, these posts may appear random, but only because they are. There is no rhyme or reason or flow to these posts. These posts will be about my friends, family, jobs, random people and my interaction with those people. I will talk about food, being fat, animals, my neighbors, poop, wiping said poop, passing gas, kissing, sexuality, picking boogers and road trips. All of the same things you interact with daily.

I mention these things because they are what make up the individual and the collective fabric of humanity. None of them are isolated. They all are interwoven to create who we are, how we think and the decisions we make. We are shaped and molded with each experience. It is up to us as individuals to live in each moment, value and reflect on the experience, and use what we learn to shape each following moment. Before you know it, you will look back on life and hopefully, find an awesome list of things that have perfected your experience here on earth.

From here on, in this book and in life, aim to live a life of lists. In this book, add to my lists. Consider how you would have handled my situation differently. Think of a similar situation you've experienced and compare your situation to mine. Shoot, I would even encourage you to go back on my posts and comment, telling me how you would have handled it and share your similar story. (That means you have to go follow me. *wink*)

In life, use the three-fold method I used in this book. In the moment, 1) absorb the story itself, then 2) point out the obvious take away and finally, 3) dig a bit deeper to identify why it resonated with you as much. I promise you. Situations you would normally breeze by will begin to grab your attention. You'll begin to be more observant of your surroundings. You'll begin to see the potential in every moment. And life will be richer because of it. Trust me. I'm living it. And hopefully, you'll see it in my lists.

Last point. (I know...I know...let's get this book started already!) I've always loved the teacher who gives you the notes or power point to their lecture. More than likely, teachers like this are more concerned with their students understanding than memorizing; interacting more than regurgitating information. For some people, regardless of the teacher's intent (See the chapter "But Did I Get An A?" in _Small Stories – Big Team_), taking notes was required in order to lock in the information. For others, it gave them an excuse to no longer pay attention in class. For the remaining few, myself included, I learned best when I could focus on the lecture and not the information. The information isn't going to change. By having the information in-hand, it freed up my brain to think instead of record. I was able to dial into the lecture which provided supplemental conversation and application that makes the information stick on the brain.

This book is those notes. This book is the power point. In the few paragraphs above, I've already told you what the class is about. There is nothing on the following pages you haven't experienced before. But I would like to provide some supplemental conversation and suggest some application along the way. So, as we move throughout this class together, free your mind to interact with the content and apply it to your life.

Okay, I'm really done this time. Let's get started.

LIST 1: PUT ON SOCKS

(April 15, 2016)

A few things I haven't been able to do well since Wednesday....

1. Wash my body.
2. Pick things up from on the floor.
3. **Put on socks.**
4. Tie my shoes.
5. Wipe. I mean...I'm getting it. Just takes a bit more effort.
6. Roll over in bed.
7. Put on a shirt.
8. Scratch my back.
9. Shoot a basketball.
10. Throw my kids around.

#Tribe #iHurt #MWIF

Jason Zielke – "Just keep it in a little perspective....It was one and half classes this week. Next week shoot for 2?"

Jeremey Fultz – "I haven't been able to do that since age 28."

Jonathan Tatum – "bro you are too funny [...]"

THE STORY

Jason is a guy I met through working at Chesapeake Energy. I worked in Chesapeake's Fitness Center coordinating member athletic activities. He was one of the regulars. His frequency naturally led to him building relationships with several of the staff in which he interacted with the most and everyone else from a distance. I was one of the distant ones with an occasional personal interaction. Eventually, Chesapeake restructured and I was laid off. I would soon start OMOS Team Building and would post my professional and personal activity on social media. Jason and I interacted loosely on social media, but nothing significant. He would comment and I would reply, but that was the extent of our interaction. I remember the first time he messaged me. It was the month after I left Chesapeake:

"Just had good thoughts of you. Hope everything is going well."

Over the course of three years, we would exchange comments and messages and the frequency of our interaction would increase. He would tell people about OMOS and what I was doing and forward potential opportunities of partnership or employment my way. It was cool and casual, until one day, he messages, "I really would like to take you to coffee one morning when you have time. I enjoy your posts and I think it would be fun. BTW, if you have a wasp problem this year, I have two bee suits." (Go watch the wasp chronicles on my page. You'll enjoy.) Within a few texts, we locked down a tee time and scheduled a round of golf for the following week.

Once we were out on the golf course, Jason tells me he ditched his morning exercise group to hang out with me. And not only were we hanging out, we were eating bad. (We ended up meeting a friend at Jason's house after the round. Over the next two hours, our diets didn't get any better.) So, as a sign of good faith and a gesture of appreciation, I offered to go to his exercise class with him the following week. Well, I knew the owner of the gym. She was glad to see me and has always tried to get me exercising regularly. She tough loves me from one visiting session into six classes over the next three weeks.

After those three weeks, I found myself sitting on the floor of my bedroom struggling to reach my feet to take my dirty socks off and again, the same position, when it was time to put clean ones back on.

THE OBSERVATION

I've shared this story with several people. Their immediate observations are very similar to mine. My body hurt! All of the routine things I normally was able to do, I couldn't do as effectively in those moments. Read the list. Those are things most people do every day with ease and simplicity. I bet many of us don't even consider the amount of effort it requires to accomplish these tasks. But here I am hurting; listening to people say my body would get used to it; that the pain would pass and I would go from hating it to loving it. Honestly, I couldn't see it. I couldn't see how it was going to happen. I couldn't predict when it would happen. And because I couldn't see it, I discontinued the exercise regimen and returned to my comfort zone of starches and carbs.

But what if I had continued? Jason would have been there to support me. The owner of the gym would have committed herself to my accountability. The regulars attending the gym and morning sessions were already learning my name and how to encourage me through my complaining. What if I would have stayed? What if I would have pressed through the discomfort? What if I viewed this moment as an opportunity instead of an obstacle? What if I would have trusted Jason, the gym owner and the process? What if...?

THE LESSON

Whether I continued or not, I still would have been able to put on my socks. The difference is how I would have been able to put on my socks and what kind of man would have been putting those socks on today. Right now, I am the heaviest I have ever been. I get tired more easily than I ever have before. I snore louder than I ever have before. My blood glucose and blood pressure are always borderline. My clothes fit tighter. I don't get to enjoy many of the physical activities I used to enjoy doing. I don't get to run around with my son as much as he or I would like. I feel a bit more self-conscious when standing and speaking in front of people...almost hypocritical, huh?

So, in that moment...on the floor...with my feet in the distance....sock in hand, I had a decision to make. I wish I could say I made the right decision or that this had been an isolated moment, but I didn't...and it isn't. I have since picked up more weight and I am faced with that moment every single morning while getting dressed. The sock in hand with the foot in the distance is a morning routine for me. In my mind, I am someone who can overcome any obstacle, accomplish any goal I set my mind to while encouraging others to do the same thing. Yet somehow, I have managed to be defeated by a sock.

It may not be a sock for you. It was for me. It may not be pride for you. It was for me. It may be trust preventing you from building successful relationships. It may be low accountability allowing you to sink back into poor decisions. It may be poor planning hindering you from being as successful as you hoped to be. It may be poor spending habits preventing you from saving to launch out on that dream or goal you set. It may be skepticism preventing you from faith. It may be past hurt keeping you from loving. It may be secrecy with others allowing you to be deceitful with yourself. Whatever it is, it's time to move on. It's time to be honest with yourself, identify the issue and press past it so you can move toward being the best you that you can be. Surround yourself with people who will encourage and love you in truth. Find people who are doing well with the thing you are doing poorly. The time is now. Put on your sock, then your shoe and run towards your goal.

List some things you have started doing to become your best self.

_____

_____

_____

_____

_____

_____

_____

_____

_____

_____

_____

_____

_____

_____

LIST 2: CHEW ON IT

(April 14, 2016)

Short list today...

1. **Heard an interesting quote yesterday that I've been struggling with. "My gift is for the world, but I (emphasis) am only for a few." Still chewing on it.**
2. I got to sit and talk with my dad this past weekend. I forget, sometimes, how much I love him.
3. My wife told me it would be disrespectful to not give her a funeral. Why do dead people even care?!?!
4. Whenever I get a chance, I like to make my kids laugh before they go to sleep. Tickles. Jokes. Anything.
5. I've been getting some pretty good feedback on #HAGD . Guess I gotta keep em coming!!!
6. I love receiving random unprovoked texts from friends. I get the warm fuzzies on the inside.
7. After leaving Tribe Gym today, I dropped something on the ground and just stared at it. It did NOT get picked up.
8. Very few things beat a hug and a compliment.
9. For two years, I worked with a kid who refused to high five me. Last week, she gave me a hug.

#MWIF

Jason Zielke – "Number 7 happens daily...That's why I gather all the laundry and put it in the washer before I go to tribe. Not picking up the floor after. Today I had trouble washing my hair...."

Amanda Williams-Siebert – "You did not pick it up. Lolololo! I started back today. It's rough but so worth it."

THE STORY

It's the end of a Saturday. I'm lying in the bed with my wife. The television is on, but it serves as background noise as neither one of us is watching it. We can hear the kids playing in the distance, but they play quietly because they know it's close to bedtime. The family Yorkie-Poo is snuggled up against my wife's feet at the end of the bed. My wife slowly strokes my shirtless belly with one hand as we both unattentively scroll social media on our phones. She breaks the silence by asking me about my day. I rattle off a few things without making eye contact or repositioning my posture towards her and continue scrolling on my phone. Subtly, the belly strokes slow to a stop and I can feel the eyes of a staring wife piercing the side of my head.

For the next few moments, she explained to me how she feels like she gets the leftover Derrick. She scrolls social media to see the smiles of others as they enjoy my company. She runs into people who talk about the wonderful conversations they've had with her husband. She gets to see pictures and videos of all this energy and charisma expended in the community. Meanwhile, she gets the watered-down version of me at home.

As I sat and listened, I couldn't deny it. I felt horrible.

THE OBSERVATION

I am the type of person who feeds on the energy of others. If others in the room lack energy, I can shift and be the spark to any conversation or any social environment. I take pride in being able to carry and sustain a social interaction with anyone in any situation. I bring energy, humor, positivity, inclusiveness and a genuine care for people everywhere I go. However, I am also the person who expends so much energy on others that quiet time is necessary to recharge. This was something I denied for a long time. I told myself I could go as long as I needed to go. However, whenever my need to recharge was brought to my attention, I would always deny it.

My wife saw it. She has always seen it. She sees it now. She sees me going and going...from person to person...from group to group. She hears about the awesome things I am doing for everyone else, but rarely able to personally attest to any of them first-hand for quite some time. Our calendar fills up with my activities months in advance, but family time or date night is rarely one of them. She and my family, were in fact, getting the leftover Derrick.

As confirmation to her observation, as we sat in church, our pastor said, "My gift is for the world, but I am only for a few." I was cut twice. First at home. Now by my pastor. I guess now, it was time to listen.

THE LESSON

I would hate to win the world and lose my family; to be considered a reliable resource in social and group dynamics, but not reflect that claim in my home. Of course, I knew that in my heart and it made sense in my head. Yet, my actions didn't show it. I see it all the time in the community, but for some reason, it didn't resonate at all with me and how it pertained to my wife and children.

Great leaders who fail at parenting. Great communicators who shut down in the presence of their spouse. Organizational gurus whose life is a mess. Doctors with bad health. Religious leaders who lose their credibility by growing unethical and immoral in their personal lives. Civil and social servants who abuse instead of protect. Teachers whose goal becomes a check and retirement instead of education and inspiration. Mentors who mis-mold and ill-advise. I don't want to be lumped in this group of people who do one thing and say another; who talk, but don't walk; who preach and not reach; who win the race, but lose the prize; who spend their entire time arriving just to forget why they were going there in the first place.

I don't want my marriage and family to be the sacrifice for my success.

That Saturday night, at the end of our conversation, my wife said something to me that has forever shaped my perspective. She said, "Sex shouldn't be the only thing that separates me from everyone else in your world. Give the world the parts of you that are for them, but save the best parts of you for me… for our children…for this home." I am still working to give my gift to the world and even more importantly, my heart to those close to me. I used to think combining them both was the only way to effective serve, but by doing so, I was slowly gaining the world, but just as slowly losing my family. As I reflect, I've determined…the success in one area and loss in another isn't worth it.

Where do you over-extend yourself? Where are you not extending yourself enough? Where does you-as-a-person stop and where does your gift or talent begin? People will mistake what you do for who you are. That's not necessarily a bad thing. To some degree, there should be some crossover or intertwining between your life and your profession, but while your gift and talent can be for the world, your heart can only be for a few. It is possible to effectively serve an organization without selling them your soul. It is possible to effective serve the community and maintain a healthy, somewhat private life. Boundaries are necessary. Boundaries are healthy. I believe the most well-rounded people have them. If you struggle in this area, try it. Draw lines. Protect time in your schedule. Have a place in your heart to which only a few people have access. You and your personal relationships will be better for it. And if you can't take me at my word, chew on it for a little bit.

List some ways you are protecting yourself in areas in which you over extend yourself.

_____

_____

_____

_____

_____

_____

_____

_____

_____

_____

_____

_____

_____

_____

_____

LIST 3: BEAUTIFUL MEMORIES

(April 10, 2016)

A few things I've learned from a weekend of soccer....

1. There are a lot of white kids named Ethan.
2. Kids love to be celebrated. Win or lose. Correction. Kids NEED to be celebrated. Win or lose.
3. A real coach coaches from beginning to end. Win or lose. I saw a coach sit down on his team because they were losing big.... even got on his phone.
4. I believe in yelling at a kid. It gets his attention and makes him understand the gravity of the moment. But when you yell all of the time, it becomes ineffective.
5. South Tulsa is beautiful!
6. **I hope we are making beautiful memories for my son. Traveling and soccer.**
7. There's no "one way" to parent a child. It's a unique blend of the parent and the child's personality. Whatever works....works.
8. Parents need other non-related adults who love their children as well.
9. American soccer needs more black children. Exposure is key.
10. I might have to get another job to support my son's soccer habit.

Tiffany Whisman – "I like that reminder, even with adults."

Brendon Williams – "These reflections are great"

Rachael Fugate – "I always thought someone needs to write a book about the things learned from 'soccer life'. There are so many valuable lessons learned ON the field and ON the sidelines."

Walela Knight – "#8 so much! I have such amazing wonderful friends who also love Trent."

THE STORY

I didn't know we would be the family to follow our kids around the country for sports. We didn't plan on it. It just kind of happened. My son has been the one we've traveled for the most. It went from community soccer (sign up and we'll put you on a team) to team soccer (we signed up with a group of people) to club soccer to competitive soccer. It was happening right before our eyes. It was snowballing downhill and we just stood in front bracing for impact…smiling the entire time. While soccer was smashing us in the face (and wallet), the only thing we could think about was how many memories he was going to have from these experiences.

Growing up, I didn't have a lot of experiences outside of my community. My wife had a few more than I did, being able to live in different places, but still nothing significant. My parents made sure I experienced a lot of things, but those experiences were all local…regional at the most. I grew up in North Tulsa (Oklahoma). Visited Kansas City once. The Dallas area is probably where we visited the most. Every now and again, we'd hit a couple of small Oklahoma towns. Essentially, my entire childhood to teen-hood was lived within a five-hour drive, absolutely nothing like my kids have and will be able to experience as they grow up. In fact, if it was up to my wife, she would have quadrupled the experiences they've already had to date.

So, for our children, what we've decide: more than food - more than stuff, we have chosen experiences.

THE OBSERVATION

My son plays on a team with other kids who have experienced more of the competitive soccer world than he has. They have played in different arenas, against better competition, stayed in crazy hotels, ate silly foods and road-tripped across the country doing so. As they share stories, you can see his eyes light up with excitement. Why?! Because he's going to be able to add to his life experiences and share in their experiences as well. Vicariously, as parents, our eyes light up when his eyes light up. Not just in sports, with anything. When he talks about astronomy, paleontology and archaeology; when he discovers something…anything new about his interests he didn't know before, his eyes light up – we light up too.

Every parent wants their children to do more, see more, experience more, eat more, travel more, learn more, save more…than they ever did or ever will. It's the cycle of life. But it's not just for "more" purposes. It's for growth and a holistic approach to life.

THE LESSON

Reading about something in a book can be categorized as an experience. Seeing it on television can be categorized as an experience. Knowing someone who has been there or has done it and hearing their stories can be considered an experience. But nothing encompasses the concept of experience like having done it yourself. When you do something yourself, that experience becomes yours. You own it. It becomes a part of who you are. It becomes a pore in your filter. It becomes a page in your chapter; a chapter in your story. There should be a huge emphasis on experiences in life.

Now, I can hear some of you screaming through the pages as you read, "Everything doesn't need to be experienced." I will admit, there is some truth to that statement, but I hope you would agree that some things DO need to be experienced. Some things can be conceptually conveyed, but there are some core things that just have to be experienced for yourself. For example: ownership. I started treating cars entirely different once I owned one. I started treating women completely different when I had a daughter. I spent money differently once I had to start using my own. I started treating electricity differently once I started paying the bill. Can I get an Amen?! (Like…why are there lights left on in rooms when no one is in there?!)

I'll say to you, GO MAKE SOME BEAUTIFUL MEMORIES! Experience life for yourself. Stop sitting on the sidelines talking about how awesome everyone else's life is. One step further, stop making excuses about how awesome your life could be if [insert whatever excuse]. Life is what you make it. You make life. You can speak life. You can mold life. You can hinder or propel life. YOU are responsible for that.

Just the other day, I met an old friend for coffee. We reminisced over the good ol' days shared at a company for which we both worked. We talked about the perks, the people, the passion, the connection amongst the employees, and the impact the company had on the community and the part we played in making all of that happen as employees. All of sudden, his demeanor shifted as he began to talk about his current job, the people, the effervescentless environment, the passionless culture and how he felt drained for pouring into a bottomless professional pit. By the time we left coffee, we had discussed his exit strategy, possible interests, combining his personal and professional gifts for maximal fulfillment and next steps towards his movement. Now that he has identified the problem and potential solutions, HE is responsible for what happens next.

Don't get stuck because of lack of options. Don't get roped in by a paycheck. Don't be frozen by indecisiveness. Flip fear the bird. Don't waste the best years of your life living for someone else. Don't chase a dream that's not yours. Do something new. Do something different. Pursue happiness without forsaking purpose. And like my son, light those eyes up and MAKE BEAUTIFUL EXPERIENCES along the way.

List some beautiful memories you have created.

_____

_____

_____

_____

_____

_____

_____

_____

_____

_____

_____

_____

_____

_____

_____

LIST 4: LOVE-HANDLES

(April 8, 2016)

Orchestra, 3rd Grade play and research presentation at my kids' school. A few things I saw/heard....

1. (Dad to son) Come on. Let's go laugh at your brother.
2. (Mom to dad) These other kids suck!
3. (Mom to daughter) You better not be the worse one.
4. (Mom in audience to daughter on stage) Smile baby!!
5. (Dad to son) I still can't believe you chose the cello.
6. (Kid to kid) Let's go play in the bathroom like we did at your house that one time.
7. (Parent to parent) Teachers should never have to pay for anything.
8. **(My wife to me) Stop rubbing my love handles.**
9. (A kid to my daughter) Your dad is so cool. (I really am!)
10. No ten today.

Sybil Burrell – "Reading these comments I think I'm a pretty cool mom for keeping my comments to myself! Lol #9"

Jaime Taylor – "10. (Derrick to self) Where's that amazing counselor at with my hug?

:-) By the way, your son was outstanding today in that play!"

THE STORY

Here we are, sitting at my kids' elementary school presentation. Over the years, my daughter has evolved into this theater girl. She has picked up tap, jazz dance, contemporary dance, hip hop, musical theater production and voice lessons. For some reason, my wife thought our daughter needed to be a bit more well-rounded and signed her up for the violin as well. And just because, as if violin and community theater weren't enough, she is also a part of the school's drama team as well. My son, on the other hand, has pretty much laid low-key at school, only dominating the educational circuit. So, during this particular assembly, he only has research on display. No biggie, right? The casual stroll by the project you helped construct…and we're out.

Now, if you have a kid, eventually, you're going to sit through numerous assemblies. You're going to be required to cheer for kids who aren't yours. You'll have to stumble through hallways of ambiguous art and pretend you know exactly what it is. Teachers will talk about projects, assignments, progress reports and give out awards and….you get where I'm going? Yeah…I feel your pain…I mean, pride. Sorry.

So, after the stroll down project lane with my son, my wife and I are sitting through this hour and a half assembly, suffering through the 80 minutes of everything else just for the 10 minutes in which our kids are involved. Naturally, being the impatient and easily distracted adult that I am, I began to observe the crowd around me. The list begins to develop. While noticing these people, I unknowingly…unconsciously begin to rub my wife's love-handles. (What are love-handles? They are the soft rolls of human waist-flesh that gently hang over the belt line.) She absolutely hates when I do this. But this time, I wasn't doing it on purpose like I normally do. It was almost like an unconscious hand movement I did to pass the time. It was almost like clicking a pen. OR how people pop their knuckles, tap their pointer fingernail on a table top or bounce their knee, which inevitably shakes the table or the floor and everyone feels it. It was an annoying fidget. I get it.

However, this time, I really wasn't trying to bother her. But I did. And she called me on it. [leaning over and aggressively whispering] "Derrick. Stop rubbing my love handles."

THE OBSERVATION

When my wife made this statement, she sincerely thought I was trying to annoy her. Had I been her, I probably would have thought the same thing. How many times have I been a pest on purpose and flicked her womanly curve? How many times have we been lying in bed and I reach over to rub her belly and make a wish? How many times has she pinched, kicked, elbowed, kneed and/or headbutted me to thwart my attempt to poke fun at something she obviously has an issue with? How many times have I seen her stand in a mirror and readjust her clothes? Or fondly stare at a high school picture? Or try on a pair of pants, only to put them back in the closet?

For her, my unconscious fidget of rubbing a sensitive area on her body was an insensitive action serving as a present and constant reminder of something with which she was obviously not pleased.

THE LESSON

How often are we offending people unknowingly? How often do we choose to not observe contextual clues? How often does someone convey displeasure and we either blow it off or minimize their perspective because we don't understand it, place the same amount of value on it or chalk it up to being their problem and not ours?

Religion. Sexuality. Gender. Rub rub rub. Race. Culture. Politics. Rub rub rub. Education. Rub. Discrimination. Rub. Oppression. Rub. Body image. Rub. Wealth disparity. Rub. Bullying. Rub. Immigration. Rub. Healthcare. Rub. Civil rights. Rub.

It's easy to not care when it's not my issue. It's easy to remain unaware when it's not knocking at my front door. What's not easy is considering my neighbor when making decisions for me. It takes effort to curb my speech and redirect my actions for the greater good of my community. It takes a conscious decision to set aside my biases and put on the perspective of another. But out of that effort and those conscious decisions, empathy and unity are groomed.

Now, I'm not talking about being politically correct. I'm not talking about softening "the truth" or adding a little sugar to the medicine. I'm not talking about beating around the bush or tip-toeing around the issue. I am saying when something rubs someone the wrong way, the person doing the rubbing should not be so quick to determine how the person being rubbed should respond. "Agh! You knew I was just playing." That shouldn't be the first thing that comes to your mind. "Quit being so sensitive!" NOPE! The list could go on, right?

All I know is, when my wife leaned over and told me to stop rubbing her love-handles, I was faced with a couple of decision. I could have told her to calm down, don't overreact and stop being so sensitive. I could have belittled her request and even followed it up with a few compliments. OR I could have acknowledged my error, apologized, legitimized her request and redirected my actions. I chose the latter....and stayed married. Ha! I'd like to think we are approaching 17 years of marriage simply because I abandoned the love-handle rub. Ha!

You are going to be faced with the same decision every single day. You will inevitably rub someone the wrong way. When you do, choose the latter.

List some awesome ways you treat your friends, family and community.

_____

_____

_____

_____

_____

_____

_____

_____

_____

_____

_____

_____

_____

LIST 5: LEND A HAND

(April 7, 2016)

Be the one that...

1. .....stands up for those who don't have a voice.
2. .....hugs in a world full of cold hand shakes.
3. .....smiles when everyone is frowning.
4. .....gives when the world takes away.
5. **.....lends a hand instead of pointing the finger.**
6. .....hopes in the time of despair.
7. ......packs on a pound just to break the skinny mold.
8. .....chooses to be pink in a world that sees black and white.
9. .....over-celebrates every single accomplishment.
10. .....gives grace because you know what it's like to not receive it.

Missy Hoppe – "YES!!! SO MANY HEARTS!!"

Tiffany Whisman – "8 and 9. Well and all of the rest too."

Robin Summers Gonzalez – "You. Just YOU Derrick Sier!!! You are awesome!"

THE STORY

I worked with a guy named Sam who acquired a unique position amongst the staff. He started out as an intern and worked his way into a part-time, then full-time position. As he joined the staff, it was clear he wouldn't really have a "thing" like everyone else, but he did have passion, excitement and was eager to do whatever was put in front of him. This means his position and associated responsibilities would be sort of a hodge-podge of leftover ideas, duties and responsibilities that didn't fit into anyone else's area. Everyone knew this going into the agreement. (Looking back, I wouldn't recommend this set-up for anyone who isn't extremely responsible and self-driven. Because of the loose lines and low definition of the position, it's almost setting someone up for either an extreme failure or enormous success. That's pretty risky.) But Sam was eager and ambitious. I'm not sure anyone else could have done the job and enjoyed it as much as Sam did. Early on, he displayed a resilient drive and creative application. However, over time, the staff started treating him as if he didn't really belong to the team. Maybe a better way to say it is, the staff started to treat him like he was the lowest and most unnecessary piece of the team. Why? Everyone else's position seemed solid and defined. Sam's appeared extra and vague.

"Hey, that's a great idea, but it doesn't fit into anything anyone else does. Let's give it to Sam." "Hey, we had some folks mention they wanted to do so-and-so. We should really do it, but we don't really have someone to coordinate that. Sam?" "Hey, Sam! Since you don't really have anything to do, can you take over this and help out with that?" "What do you mean you're busy?! All you do is blah." "Surely you can put that on hold and help us out. I mean, it's only such-and-such." "Hey, Sam! Come do this. I'm sure your project can wait." It's sad and embarrassing to admit, but at times, I caught myself contributing to the ill-treatment of Sam and his position.

Sam went from excited and eager to confused to discouraged to defensive to resentful to angry to quitting.

THE OBSERVATION

What started out as excitement, eventually ended in Sam leaving his position within the group. It wasn't a pretty transition either. It was messy. Understandably so. Sam got fed up. When he took the position, he knew there would be some challenges along the way, but he thought those challenges would come from outside the group, not inside.

He enjoyed the miscellaneousness of his job. He enjoyed the freedom created by undefined lines and ambiguous borders. He did not like being treated as if his responsibilities and contributions to the staff were minimal and unnecessary; as if they didn't matter. This caused Sam to start saying NO to new projects. He started saying NO to assisting others with their programming. His frustration caused him to become distant, grumpy, short, non-compliant, confrontational and a paycheck player, all because of the way his co-workers treated him.

Sam felt like everyone around him was pointing the professional finger instead of lending him a professional hand.

Now, there is a lot to be said about assumptions based on the acts of others. I'm sure if Sam went from co-worker to co-worker and asked if they thought less of his position and contribution to the staff, they would have all denied it; myself included. But that's not what the actions of the staff conveyed to Sam. The words said, "We are glad to have you on board. We are excited about what you bring to the team." The actions said, "Your contribution is minimal. Your position is expendable. We are possibly slightly better with you around, but only because of your ability to make our programs look better." Very few people are able to stay in a position with such conflicting support. Especially someone like Sam.

THE LESSON

When conflict breaks out, what causes people to point the finger of blame instead of lending a hand of resolution? When people are singled out for their participation or lack thereof, what causes those people to identify what others are doing or not doing without the intent of helping? It happens all the time. We are quick to point out issues and slow to resolve them. In Sam's case, the staff had several options. They could have not hired Sam and broken up the straggling responsibilities amongst the existing staff. They could have allowed Sam to stumble through the process of solidifying his position. OR they could have hired Sam and given him the support and tools he needed to best succeed. And this is what lending a hand instead of pointing a finger looks like. My gosh! I can only imagine the potential that could have been unleashed from within Sam had any of these options been explored.

You may not be able to pick up every piece of trash, but you can start by picking up one. Don't just point at the trash and keep walking. Don't just complain about all the litterers. Don't just complain about the trashman and the inefficient and messy way he gets trash from your bin to the dumpster. Do something. Lend a hand. Heck, do both! Complain AND do something. But by doing nothing, nothing changes. Well, that's untrue. The situation will change. It will get worse. Trash will pile up on the sidewalks and streets while people point and complain…waiting on someone to fix the problem while we move along to whatever else we deem is important, when the resolution lies within our grasp.

Don't just complain about legislation. Vote. Get involved. Don't just complain about "kids these days". Mentor. Raise the children closest to you to be world changers. Don't just complain about today's music. Make good music. Support the people whose music you enjoy. Stop complaining about your spouse and work to reconcile and rekindle. Stop complaining about your job and pursue something you love. Don't continue to look in the mirror and be disappointed with your weight. Start exercising. Change your eating habits. Stop whining about your boring life. Step outside the box. Expand your experience. Do things you don't normally do. Attach yourself to people who are going places and doing things you want to do. Because if you don't…if WE don't, things that started out good will get worse. Things we were passionate about will lose its savor. Our zeal will fizzle. All because we settled for pointing the finger, instead of lending a hand…at people, at situations, at ourselves.

Get involved. Be a mover. Be a shaker. Lend a hand. Don't just sit back and point a finger at life.

List some ways you lend a hand to your friends, family and community.

_____

_____

_____

_____

_____

_____

_____

_____

_____

_____

_____

_____

_____

_____

LIST 6: MY NEIGHBOR ASKED

(April 6, 2016)

A few random moments over the past couple of weeks...

1. I saw a squirrel and bird eating from the same pile of food. Is that normal?
2. I saw a toddler casually flicking her mother's nipple in the food court at the mall. Mom didn't seemed phased.
3. **My neighbor asked if I needed to borrow his mower. LOL!**
4. I asked a kid why was he fighting. He said. "Because it's Thursday."
5. I took my UCO students to FD Moon elementary. One of the Moon kids said, "Who all these white people?!?"
6. I had a friend sit in my driveway and talk to me in his car for two hours on a Tuesday night. I don't take that lightly.
7. I think my love language has switched from touch to words of affirmation.
8. I've read three books in two weeks.
9. I hugged a kindergarten girl. She said, "Dang, you smell good!" *neck roll* *hands on hips*
10. I yelled at a ref this past weekend. I was ashamed. It really was a bad call tho.
11. Someone recognized me as the "body roll guy from poetry night".

#MWIF

Jennifer Bridges – "These. Never. Get. Old. Ever!"

Jerry MrWill Williams – "Wonderfully random as always"

Jaime Taylor – "[...] #7. That's not allowed to happen. I like hugging you too much. Oh, and these posts are always awesome (there an affirmation, just in case)."

Rachel Clapp – How lucky are we to know you? #blessed #youisawesome :-)"

Barry Bergstrom – "It was a bad call. You weren't the only good parent yelling. You're an amazing man and I'm thankful to have you in my life."

THE STORY

Oscar is my neighbor. He's in his mid to late sixties. He has children my age. He is always well put together; shirt pressed and tucked into nice jeans or khakis. Oscar and his wife, Minnie, bought the lot next to their house so they could build and work a garden. It was their way of staying active, contributing to their own physical and psychological health and more than likely, giving themselves some space to breath since the houses were so closely built together. Oscar bought his house when the neighborhood was being built. So, he and his wife are one of the few remaining original homeowners in the community. Oscar's wife is retired. He is self-employed and soon approaching retirement. When Oscar isn't working his garden, he is picking up nuts from his acorn tree (he doesn't like the squirrels in his yard or the wear and tear on his mower), he's trimming his tree, cutting his grass, edging his bushes, fixing his fence or repairing something on his house. Oscar and Minnie live a pretty low-key lifestyle, but active none-the-less.

One day, after a few back to back hard rains, I mustered up the motivation to cut my front yard. For some reason, I let the yard get away from me. I could tell it had gotten away from me because whenever I was outside, the neighbors would give me the "aren't you going to cut your grass" look whenever they drove by. I wasn't happy about it either. I knew it had to be done. I just didn't want to be the one to do it. It had gotten out of hand and I knew it was going to be a beast of a project. I admit. It was bad. It was so bad that people with lawn mower businesses started to leave hand-written notes on our screen door. It was so bad that things started to grow I didn't even know I had. Random flowers had begun to bloom everywhere. I found my neighbor's mail in there along with a couple of nests. It was bad.

So, I throw on a random set of clothes from the dirty clothes basket and stumble to the garage. I lift the garage door, drag the mower out to the driveway, give it a few yanks in an attempt to start it, but it wouldn't start. By now, Oscar hears me struggling and comes out to see if he can help…because that's just how he is. After a few more attempts, I get frustrated and roll my mower back into the garage. I come back out to shake Oscar's hand and say 'thank you' for helping. While shaking my hand, Oscar pushing his glasses up his nose a bit, glances at my yard as says, "Are you sure you don't wanna use my mower?" (On top of him being a really nice guy, I'm pretty sure he also thought I was going to give up, go back in the house and not cut my grass for another week.) I replied, "Oscar, you don't think I'm going to cut my yard, do you?" He said, "Well, Derrick. I believe you'll get to it eventually, but now is just as good a time as any. Let me grab my mower and we'll knock it out together." I said, "You know what, Oscar? I'm going to do it. Matter of fact, I'll do it right now. And I'll do the whole yard with my weed eater."

Oscar tried to talk me out of it, but I was stubborn and bullheaded and actually, kind of offended. Two hours later, the yard was cut. It wasn't pretty, but it was chopped down. I raked and bagged the wreckage. I put the bags on the side of the house. And before I pridefully strolled my arrogant self into the garage, I looked toward Oscar and gave him a polite and passive "I told you so" wave. I put up the weed eater. Took a shower, during which every muscle in my body cramped up. I mean completely locked up. I ended up falling asleep on the floor in a towel and would eventually physically pay for that decision over the next three days.

THE OBSERVATION

I wonder what I looked like to the other neighbors that were looking on?

First, they notice the grass getting taller. Then they see the flowers growing and wildlife inhabiting the place. They see me come home, leave, check the mail and repeat; all the while, walking and driving past the grass that's so obviously annoying to everyone else. Then, they see me finally pull out the mower. I crank the mower, but it doesn't start. They watch in dismay. I try again, but it doesn't start. Out of nowhere, Oscar comes to save the day. The onlookers get excited as hope for a well-kept neighborhood still looms in the distance. However, Oscar can't fix the mower. The mower goes back into the garage. Oscar and I shake hands. Oscar walks away. The neighbors reach for the phone to call the city to report a home with high grass, but wait....I emerge from the garage with a...a......weed eater?!

Half of the neighbors watch in disappointment. The other half watch for entertainment.

THE LESSON

Stubbornness can really cramp your lifestyle. That was cheesy. I know, but it's true. Instead of taking the advice and help offered to me, I chose to prove a point that didn't even need proving. Here I have someone offering to not only let me use his mower, but he was going to physically help me cut my grass as well. Even more so, I wonder how many times Oscar simply thought about offering to help with my yard before he actually came over. Maybe he didn't even want to initially physically help. Maybe he just wanted to say something. Offer advice. Offer his mower. Offer the number of a friend who cuts yards. Fix my mower. Check to see if everything was okay with the family and work. As someone who genuinely cared, he probably didn't know exactly what to do, but knew something needed to be done. When he heard me trying to start my mower, he took advantage of the opportunity.

Which brings me to this. There are two sides to this

situation. The giver and the taker. The person offering and the person receiving.

From the taker's/receiver's side, I'd like to think I'm the type of guy that is receptive, open and welcoming to feedback, but maybe that wasn't the vibe I gave my neighbors. Which causes me to ask a couple of questions. What could I have done to make them feel more comfortable with approaching me? Had they offered something in the past I didn't accept? Did I say something that gave them an un-receptive perception in our HOA meetings? Was I brash or coarse in our interactions? Had I offered them bad advice before? Had I mishandled our relationship in any capacity?

From the giver's/offerer's side, what makes us say something? What makes us not say anything? Are we waiting to see if that person will work it out themselves? Are we afraid of possibly being hurt or hurting their feelings? Do we not have the access or relationship enough to say anything at all? Are we mis-perceiving and misunderstanding their tone and personality? Do we even care enough to go out of our way to say something? Do we believe that once we offer the assistance, we are now obligated to make sure it comes to pass? Is it easier for everyone to simply worry about themselves?

I can't imagine what it took for Oscar to come over and say something to me. What I do know is that I didn't take the advice or help he offered, which I should have. Because I didn't and the way I refused it, that was the last time he ever offered it.

I strive to be the type of person people will bend over backwards to help. I want loyal and consistent helpers. I want people who will go out of their way to assist me. I want people who come up with creative ways to help me. I want people to think about how they can help me without me asking them. And while I may not accept or apply what was given, I want people to feel free to offer it. No one makes it on their own. No one has ever made it on their own. Even more so, I'm not trying to be the first to do it. I want help. I need help. I solicit help. Without help, I could have never become what I am today. Without help, I will never reach my fullest potential.

Who are you helping? Who have you offered your mower to lately?

List some areas in which you allow people to help you.

_____

_____

_____

_____

_____

_____

_____

_____

_____

_____

_____

_____

_____

_____

LIST 7: HIGHS AND LOWS

(March 23, 2016)

A few topics I've covered with friends in the last week:

1. Do you spray then wash your hands or vice versa?
2. Politics. Is there currently a "right" choice?
3. Starting a business together.
4. **Marriage: working thru the highs and lows.**
5. Dudes taking high angle selfies.
6. Historical and theological accuracy of the Christian Bible.
7. Why DO opposites attract?
8. Techniques to properly smoking meats (types of meat, wood, seasonings, temperature and length of time.)
9. The anti-sexiness of a 9-to-5.
10. Are full-frontal hugs appropriate?
11. Gender roles.
12. Fear the Walking Dead or Game of Thrones?!?! Record one? Watch the other live?
13. Budget cuts for schools happening at the same time as the state capital is being repaired. $125 million dollar decision.
14. Apple vs Android
15. Israel Houghton.

Missy Hoppe – "I had a 'Derrick' moment today!! I thought of you!

Joshua Pease – "I am gonna start recording my 'Derrick' moments"

Amy Parker – "Full frontal hugs are not just appropriate, they are needed!"

Billie Smith – "A friend of my daughter's recently said, 'you guys ask a lot of questions.' Man, we don't know how to skim the surface. These lists make my day"

THE STORY

Talking to people isn't an issue for me. I can talk to anyone. Heck, I talk to myself all the time. This book is a great example. I've sat down with a laptop and poured out my thoughts to anyone and everyone who will read this. Sure, I've bounced the thoughts off a few of my closest friends. Sure, I've met with mentors, coaches, executives and consultants about what I want to say, what I want to convey and how I'd like my readers to respond. But at the end of the day, I'm hashing it all out by myself. I have to sit down and talk out loud while I type to make sure the thoughts coming out of my head and heart are conveyed correctly on the screen. I have that process locked down.

Talking to my wife, on the other hand, takes preparation.

I don't know what it is about sitting across from her. Shoot, we don't have to be sitting. We could be laying in bed. I could be on the floor, while she's in the bed – no eye contact. She could be on the other side of the door. We could be yelling down the street at each other. She could be in another country… in another time zone and we're talking on the phone…and talking to her about our highs and lows can still be difficult.

I don't know if I want to appear to have everything in control. I know I definitely don't like confrontation. I hate the way our family feels when the air is thick with offensive and that icky uncomfortable tension. I don't know if I think she will view me differently. I don't know if my thoughts and assumptions are clear…if they are even correct. I could be making small things into big things. I don't know if this is something that will blow over if left unaddressed OR will it dig deeper and grow bigger if we don't nip it in the bud right now. I generally....just don't know.

That's why I am thankful for friends who will discuss the high and lows of marriage with me.

They bring a calm to the situation and reassure me that love, grace, understanding and transparency conquers all fear and builds great rapport. These are all things my wife and I have invested in each other for years, which means, we have a lot of those things stored up for times when the air is thick with offensive and icky uncomfortable tension. I'm grateful for friends that are invested in my success and push me to be the greatest that I can be in all areas of my life...in this case, marriage.

THE OBSERVATION

Have you ever seen a hot air balloon? It's constructional and operational archaicity is fascinating. The simplicity of what happens to a balloon when the air inside it is heated and cooled - astonishing. The security of the traditional wicker basket – classic. The knowledge, understanding and use of layered wind currents to control the distance and direction of the craft – phenomenal. The outdated functionality of sand bags serving as assisted weight and speed control – stunning. And yet, the wonder experienced when riding a hot air balloon consists of a little hot air, cold air and a breeze blowing from here to there.

Such is the marriage. There are so many things which impact the flow and flight of a life spent with someone else. Some people will look at the hot air balloon and think of every reason to not participate. Others will look at it and see the opportunity of a life time. Those questions are irrelevant for me now because I've gotten on the balloon with a pretty lady and we've been riding this thing for years. During this ride, we pump a lot of hot air in the balloon and it feels like we could safely reach the stars. Other times, the air chills and it seems as if we may quickly and painfully crash. I bet there have been times when both of us were looking over the edge of the basket wondering why we got on this thing in the first place. Is it possible to get off and not finish the ride? How hard would it actually hurt if we jumped from this distance? Would I be better off living with the pain and injury of jumping than a life safe in the basket with him/her? There have even been times when we have retreated to the farthest possible opposite corners of the basket and thought "I'm not coming out of the corner until they apologize or the ride is over."

But something happens when we are reminded of our commitment to each other. When we lock eyes and see the core of the person to whom we made promises. Something rekindles the fire when we are able to put things into the right perspective. And while I wish we could take credit for, under our own power and desire, being able to lure ourselves back into the center of the basket to enjoy the rest of the ride on this hot air balloon of marriage, we can't. Our friends and family have definitely played their part. They held true to the vows they made to us...as we made them to each other. Every reminder. Every encouraging word. Every reassuring hug. Every poke and nudge that pushed us back towards each other. It has all worked for the good of our marriage.

THE LESSON

Life lifts you. Life grounds you. Good friends help you navigate. And I know the term "good" is subjective from person to person. For some, a good friend may be the person who holds your hair out of the toilet while you throw up. They may be the person who lends you money or allows you to borrow their clothes. They may be the type of person who tells you that your breath stinks and picks food out of your teeth. They could be the type of person who drops you off at the airport early in the morning, pick you back up late at night, helps you change your tire and brings you gas when your car runs out for the fourth time. Those are all friends.

You should also have friends with whom you can dream and share your fears. They should be able to remind you of your greatness. They should be a shoulder on which you can cry and also let you know when enough crying has taken place. They should be able to tell you to stop whining and boss up. They should push you when you feel like quitting. They should run the marathon of life WITH you and not just cheer from the sidelines. You should have friends who stand in front of the door when you want to leave. They should hug and discipline your children when you're not around. They should be able to carry your weight when you're weak and fly with you when it's time for you to soar.

The word "friend" shouldn't be thrown around lightly. They have a huge responsibility. I expect a lot from the people to whom I give that title. You should have a similar standard as well. You're worth it. Sure, you can be great by yourself. But you will never reach your greatest potential without the exponential factor of friendship included into the equation of your life. And anyone not meeting your standard of friendship needs to either be redefined or find other people to which their level of friendship matches the requirement.

List some ways you plan on being a better friend.

_____

_____

_____

_____

_____

_____

_____

_____

_____

_____

_____

_____

_____

LIST 8: EAR HAIR

(March 21, 2016)

I fear....

1. Liking the same picture on Twitter, Instagram AND Facebook.
2. Passing gas in my car and hoping it airs out before I give someone a ride.
3. Turning the faucet water on too high, splashing my crotch and people thinking I didn't shake well.
4. **Forgetting to shave my ear hair.**
5. Seeing a social media friend in real life and not recognizing them and/or not remembering their name. Especially if I recently "liked" or "commented".
6. Bad breath. My own and someone else's.
7. That awkward pause when I don't hear what someone said, but then I laugh like it was a joke, but it was actually a question. And it makes it seem like I wasn't actually listening to what they were saying.
8. My card not working "properly" in the check-out line...AND I have a bang of groceries.
9. Sending food back when it wasn't prepared the way I asked. #nospitplz
10. Booty-crack sweat when I've been sitting too long. Hot days + Poor circulation = Big boy problems...

#mwif

Jenn Fitts Higgins – "I just heart you, friend!!"

Marika Chambers – "I am cracking up!!!"

Carmon Williams – "I really really want u to know these posts make me smile on m tough days lol #3! #8 happened to me! I laughed so hard reading this!"

THE STORY

I was getting ready for an event. It was a formal event. I did NOT want to go, but I felt like I had to for multiple reasons. When it comes to formal events, five-year-old Derrick starts to squirm and appear in the form of an adult. I just simply did NOT want to go to this event. Why? I don't prefer formal events because of how stuffy they feel. The air feels stuffy. My collar is rubbing my neck. The tie is always too tight. The conversations seem shallow…and stuffy. The chairs seem to sit differently. I walk differently. I sit and stand differently. The formality of the table setup makes you eat differently. I don't even breath the same when I'm in a formal attire. Stand up, button the jacket. Sit down, unbutton the jacket. Lean in for a bite of food, tuck the tie. Come out of the restroom, tuck the shirt. Formal handshake. Disingenuous laugh. Repeat. Go home. Did I mention I don't like…I don't prefer formal events? I don't. (You don't have to say it. Grow the heck up, son. – But, in this case, I didn't want to.)

I got my suit cleaned and shirt pressed at the cleaners. Shined my shoes. Replaced the tattered belt. Cut my hair, as I often do myself. Trimmed my facial hair. Showered. Put on my good underwear. (Ha!) Put on the newly acquired colorful socks given to me by a friend. A couple of swipes of deodorant. A few squirts of cologne. Tied one of the best knots I've ever tied on a tie. The wife is concluding her two-hour preparation process with make-up, accessories and the locating and packing of an extra pair of pre and post event car shoes. We get to the car, drive to the location and park. She leans over to put the final touches on my shirt collar and tie, and says, "Why didn't you cut you ear hair?"

Me: "Ear hair? I have ear hair?"

Wife: "Uhh, yeah."

Me: "Like, you can see it just sitting there?"

Wife: "Uhhh, yeah."

Me: "How long have I had it?"

Wife: "That doesn't matter right now. Why didn't you cut it?"

Me: "I obviously....never mind."

I don't remember much else from that night. However, I do remember watching the eyes of everyone I encountered, wondering if they were also noticing my ear hair.

THE OBSERVATION

I don't really look in the mirror often. Mirrors are used to get things done, not for reflection. Period. It's not healthy to spend a lot of extra time searching and observing what has happened to the face and body over the years. It's not wise examining what is currently there. And you should definitely not disappoint yourself by standing in the mirror trying to figure out the future; regretting what has happened, what is happening and what could possibly be. Nope. I'm not a mirror guy. Never have been. Make sure your clothes are not wrinkled. Brush your teeth. Move on. Or so I thought....

Over the years, people are taught to attach mirrors with the concept of vanity. For the people who look a mess, we ask them, "Have you looked in a mirror lately?" ...implying they need to see, be just as disappointed in and change the things we are observing about them. For the people who spend too much time in the mirror, we say, "Stop spending so much time in that mirror!" If it's someone who doesn't like what they see, we tell them they are beautiful and perfect. If it's someone who is trying to make sure their perfection is maintained throughout the day, we call them vain and shallow. As a result, people don't understand the proper amount of mirror time. Their relationship with the mirror is nonexistent or compulsive with very few finding the sweet spot where proper mirror usage is found.

The same with internal reflection. Look around you. I bet you are able to identify the people who spend too much time in the mirror. They overthink themselves. They need people to tell them they are okay and beautiful and smart because they spend too much time noticing the bad that they miss out on the good. They want to appear a certain way more than they actually want to be what people perceive. They probably also suffer from indecisiveness and live according to the expectation of others. On the other hand, I'm sure you can identify the people who don't spend any time in their internal mirror. What about the people that spend a proper amount of time reflecting over their decision making and how they appear to others? Are those people confident in themselves? Are they painfully aware of their limitations and opportunistically aware of their qualities and strengths? Do they show compassion because they acknowledge their own flaws and imperfections?

Look around. You'll see it. Look within. You'll see it there too.

THE LESSON

Lately, I've been spending a lot of time in the mirror. Yes, the physical mirror. But even more so, my life mirror. I stare and ask hard questions. Do I like what I see? What changes need to be made? How have I become the person looking back at me in that reflection? What are my flaws? What are some things I like about myself? Not because I'm vain or self-absorbed, but because I haven't spent much time in the mirror lately. I've been so busy relying on what others see me as and not enough time confirming if that's what or who I want to be. And maybe it's more comfortable to rely on the perception of others rather than taking a peek for myself. And maybe if I peek, over time, I will grow comfortable with what I see in the mirror...with whom I see in the mirror. And maybe I haven't been...and that's the reason I haven't spent much time in the mirror until now. Maybe I was afraid of seeing something and as long as I didn't know it was there, I wasn't able to be distracted enough to care to fix it. And that works if everyone around me continues to play the ignorance game with me... if everyone continues to participate in my delusion. But the moment someone points something out, it's now on me to find a mirror and correct it. Because, in all truth, if I spent any significant time in the mirror, I would have seen it too.

List some awesome things you notice about yourself when looking in the mirror.

_____

_____

_____

_____

_____

_____

_____

_____

_____

_____

_____

_____

_____

_____

LIST 9: COOL PEOPLE

(March 16, 2016)

A few random things that have happened over the past few weeks....

1. **Committed to memorize my local Wal-Mart cashiers' names. Jacob and Stephanie are pretty cool people.**
2. Helped a lady who ran out of gas.
3. Helped an older couple. Their car broke down in the middle of the street.
4. Pulled my neighbor's trash can from the curb to his house.
5. Attended a neighborhood movie night. This guy pulled out a 10-foot screen and provided popcorn for his entire block!
6. Grilled some wings and took my friend a few so he could enjoy my grilly goodness.
7. Helped my kids in their garden.
8. Played defense on my friend's son as he ran routes in the park.
9. Rolled the windows down, turned up some Selena Gomez and sang super loud with my kids.
10. Received a 'thank you' text from one of my students. Teachers really do have an impact.

Show love. Have fun. Smile a bunch. Touch people's heart.

Brie A. Reynolds – "Derrick Sier is a great man! A true inspiration of manhood and authenticity."

Amanda Williams-Siebert – "#1. You're so awesome."

Melissa Jones Chunu – "You're awesome!!!! Great inspiration!!!!!!"

Ashley Neely – "You rock!"

Bryant Andrews Jr. – "You at Walmart too much lol"

Joshua Pease – "This, I need to strive to be like this."

Missy Hoppe – "I want to follow you around one of these days. I love your stories!"

THE STORY

Wal-Mart is right around the corner from my house. It's less than a mile. It's a neighborhood market, so not your super market kind of Wal-Mart. The store is smaller, which means fewer aisles, fewer checkout lanes and fewer employees. In addition to the store being a smaller environment, I completed my grocery shopping at night. As it pertains to the employees, this narrowed the number of workers I interacted with during my shopping. This is where Jacob and Stephanie enter the picture.

Stephanie is a young lady who dates the guy working as cashier two lanes down from her. They occasionally glance over at each other and smile or wink while completing their duties at the cash register. She just moved out of her mom's home to live on her own. Her dad hasn't been in the picture for quite some time. She has only one sibling. She wants to go back to school. She drives a used car for which she paid cash. She hasn't bought any new clothes in an entire year. Her favorite color is pink and our birthdays are in the same month. She doesn't want to work at Wal-Mart forever, but working over night fits her day schedule dream of finishing school so she can start a normal life of adulthood.

Jacob is a father of two. He loves cooking for his family and watching his children play sports. Outside of Wal-Mart, he has a few side-gigs to supplement his children's distant future plans for college, marriage and entrepreneurship. In fact, our kids used to attend the same school...same grade. I also remember seeing Jacob with his family at school. I remember seeing him at Wal-Mart, but I don't know why it took me so long to make the two separate people...the same person. When I brought it up, Jacob said, "I enjoyed how whenever you saw me at Wal-Mart, you spoke as if you knew me from a different life, but didn't know which life it was." I felt so embarrassed. Jacob's smile is pure and his conversation is warm.

Whenever I do my grocery shopping, I only go to Jacob or Stephanie.

THE OBSERVATION

My wife and I go back and forth on traveling. Well, not really. We both know where the other stands on traveling. She wants to go. I don't. Pretty simple, right? Well, it's not. In fact, until recently, it has been a pretty sore spot in our marriage. My wife dreams of traveling the world. She has this vision board on the wall next to our head board. It reads, "I'm in love with places I've never been before....". She wants to go! Where?! Everywhere! And not the touristy places. She wants to visit the hole in the wall, lost in the forest, dilapidated bridge crossing, non-English speaking, health code violating, dirt road having, no-wifi receiving, mosquito virus carrying, bring your own drinking water, get there on a paddle-boat places...to which I have NO desire to go.

But because of our lines of work, I get to travel often and she doesn't. As if that wasn't a jab in the gut for my wife, I often add injury to insult by complaining every time I have to go somewhere. Can you imagine dying of hunger and seeing people throw away food? OR dying of thirst and seeing people pour it down the sink or flush it down the toilet? (This really does happen, by the way...that's for another book, but I won't write it.) This is how my wife feels when I complain about traveling. How has she made it this long?!

Outside of the hassle of getting to those locations, the real reason I don't like to travel is because I don't like being in places where I don't know people. If I know people who know the area, I immediately feel exponentially more comfortable than had I been dropped in a city with only Google as my guide. Comfort, hands down, is the driving force of my social nature. I need to make every place as familiar as possible for me. And part of me being comfortable is knowing people. Selfish, I know.

THE LESSON

I hate Wal-Mart. I don't like shopping there. However, Jacob and Stephanie significantly improve my shopping experience. I hate traveling, especially to new places where I don't know people. However, if I knew people in those new places, I would feel significantly more comfortable than had I been dropped in a random place.

For me, people are the common denominator in every significant experience in my life. The cooler the people, the cooler the experience. I've disliked several jobs, but the people made those jobs bearable. I despise going to hospitals, but they're a lot cooler when the staff is pleasant. I do not like driving long distances, but the drive is a heck of a lot better when I have good company riding, seat dancing and laughing with me. I can be spiritual by myself, but joining my faith with other like-spirited individuals enhances the journey.

Stephanie and Jacob were probably just doing their jobs. I bet they do for others all day, what they did for me in those late-night shopping hours. To them, it probably wasn't even special. I'm not even sure they would recall our encounters with the same fondness. But at the end of the day, regardless of the experience, everyone everywhere will eventually need a Jacob or Stephanie. And if we are aware enough in those same situations, we can probably be a Stephanie or Jacob for someone else like me...struggling in the moment and needing a pretty cool person as home base to make them feel comfortable.

List some ways in which you make people feel safe.

_____

_____

_____

_____

_____

_____

_____

_____

_____

_____

_____

_____

_____

_____

LIST 10: WHAT YALL DOING IN HERE?!

(March 8, 2016)

Why do I feel like my investigative skills have increased since having children?!?!

1. Did you have homework last night? Then what's this paper I found balled up in the bottom of your backpack?!
2. How did you take a shower and the soap still dry... towel ain't even wet.
3. How you wipe well and it was only two squares on the roll?!?! How do I know it was only two squares left?! Don't worry about that!
4. Bruh...trust me. You did not brush your teeth this morning! Breath smelling like draws! Toothbrush ain't wet. Not a drop of water on the sink.
5. So uuhhhh, who is [insert name I've been hearing said a bunch during kid talk]?!
6. **Hay!! *bust in door* What yall doing in here?! It's too quiet!**
7. **Hay! *bust in door* What yall doing in here?! It's too loud!!!**
8. I know you ate the last of the pizza! What's that stain on your shirt?!? And I can smell it on your breath!
9. Did you ask your momma the same question you asked me after I said no?!
10. If I go in here...and this room ain't clean. Boooooooy! *walks in* *room is clean* Pick that paper clip up....

Jessica Nilsen – "I love your posts! They brighten my day!!! Parenting is detective work for sure!"

Kelda S. Slater – "Yaaasss! I think I've said all of these to the seven year old!"

Monica Stephens – "Thank God!!! It's not just my kids! LOL"

Phillis Tyson – "Love it. You have to be quick on your feet with children…so I've heard"

Cessnie Shelton – "Derrick Sier you are so CRAZY! But sir you must be a fly on the wall in my house. Too Funny!"

Judie Lavender – "LOL cause they make us do that LOL"

THE STORY

Growing up, when it came to playing and having fun, we had adults' rules and we had the kids' rules. A few of the standard adult rules:

1. If there is an argument, find a way to resolve it or I will resolve it for you. If I have to come in there, everyone is going to have to quit playing that particular game and come inside, find something else to do or I'm going to spank someone and tell them, "now stop crying, wash your face, go back outside and get to playing."
2. Don't hit your sister. If she hits you, tell me or find something else to play that won't make her mad.
3. The older kids look out for the younger kids. If the younger kids get hurt, whoever was the oldest and in charge will answer to me and/or everyone had to find something else to do.
4. Don't play house.
5. Don't play church.
6. If anyone starts crying, I will come in and make everyone else cry.
7. If you break anything or anyone, the person who did the breaking gets a spanking, then everyone has to

go home and/or come in and find something else to do.

8. Don't play in your good clothes.
9. Get all of your homework and chores done before playing.
10. If you are playing inside, you have to play quiet and with the doors open.
11. None of the kids....have any kids, so no one should be "bossing" anyone else.
12. Don't make me get up out of this chair.

Then there were the kids' rules:

1. If you cheat, don't get caught....and then tell your best friend how to do it.
2. Pay attention to the street light. It's the difference between being able to play tomorrow or in two weeks.
3. It doesn't matter what's going on, you better hear your parents call your name.
4. If you break something, try to fix it. If you can't fix it completely, fix it enough to where the next person who touches it....breaks it.
5. If you're losing at a game, either act confused about the rules or suggest an amendment that favors your ability to participate well.
6. Even numbered teams work best. Any-many-miny-moe...preferably. That way, no one has to sit out.
7. Know your parent well enough to allow or prevent your friends from asking your parents for permission FOR YOU to do anything. Depending on the parent, you may get the benefit of them caving into kid-pressure by putting them on the spot OR your parent may tell your friend no...and then proceed to embarrass you for having them ask and your friend for actually asking.
8. "Please don't tell!" and "I'm sorry!" should be a part of everyone's vocabulary, even if they don't mean it. It's for the sake of the group.
9. After coming inside from playing, make sure you

wash your hands before going into the fridge.

10. While the odds are slim, you may get a yes (and then in trouble) if you ask the other parent after the first parent says no.

11. Stay away from the person who's not afraid to do anything and the person who is afraid to do everything. Hang with the people in the middle.

12. If we are all going to lie, make sure everyone has the same lie and willing to tell and repeat said lie.

However, the advantage always goes to the adult. Why? The adult has been a child before, but the child has never been an adult before. The adults have come through a long line of rule adjustments and playing evolution. The games may change, but the motive stays the same. That means, the adults are aware of the rules way before the children. Now, the children will eventually learn, but they must first navigate the art of playing and the rules associated with doing so, while expanding their experience within those set of rules. This means testing the waters and being corrected in the process.

I was no exception to the rule. In fact, one of the ways I learned when I was breaking the rules was when my dad would open the closed door to a room that we were playing in OR he would walk into an open room and the first thing he would say is, "What's going on here? Yall too quiet." Or he would say, "What's going on in here? Yall making too much noise." Eventually, through questions and corrected behavior, we learned the rules and created our own set of rules to navigate those rules.

THE OBSERVATION

One of the strange things about these rules is that many of them where never verbally addressed. Regarding the adult rules, the kids were never sat down and briefed before play. They sort of learned on the fly. The same with the kid rules. There was no pre-game meeting to discuss the social nature of fun that was about to be had. The game rules were always addressed, but rarely the social rules surrounding the game.

Social rules meaning, it only took Mr. Johnnie one time to come running out of his house, stand on the porch and load his gun for everyone to remember not to play in his yard. It only took mom one time to throw her shoe for everyone to know to be quiet while her stories were on TV. The same with dad and his tools; they were not toys...keeping in mind, Dad never told us we couldn't play with his tools. We just mentally noted, forever branded in our minds, his response when he caught us playing swords with his wrenches. The girls learned that when boys were mean, they liked you. The boys eventually learned the infamous cooties were quite pleasant to catch, contrary to popular belief.

Learning from the responses around you and from the experiences of others has always been a solid way to "learn the rules". And when it came to us, as kids, placing certain rules and social cues in context, many corrective and learning experiences began with, "Hey! What yall doing in here?!"

THE LESSON

Sure, it would be easier, smoother...more efficient if the low-down...the skinny...the rules were given right up front, but sometimes, it doesn't happen that way. In fact, I would be willing to bet the most important lessons anyone ever learns come primarily through observation. Why? Observation fills in the gray. It's the mortar in between the brick. The meat of the sandwich. The heart behind the statement. Being able to observe well fills in the gaps between what was said and what was intended. Observation moves past the letter of the law and into the heart of the structure it aims to provide. And after years of practice as a child...as a teenager...as an adult, husband, father, friend, business man...I am still afforded the wonderful opportunity to continue to play this wonderful game of life and practice more along the way through observation.

So, when we were playing in the bedroom and something hit the floor really loud and my mother said, "Don't make me get up out of this chair!" That meant she has been working all day and she's tired. Not only did she hold down a full-time job, but she added to her list of responsibilities daily by cleaning up after me, my dad and the dogs, prepping several meals and being an active church and community member. By the time she was able to sit in a chair, take her shoes off, eat some food and watch a bit of TV before she had to finish the rest of her chores, take a shower, tend to me, get in bed and start all over tomorrow, the last thing she wanted to do was mediate play time, discipline children and fix a broken piece of furniture that she spent her hard earned money purchasing for me. But keep in mind, this is today-Derrick reflecting on then-Derrick. I didn't have the ability to mortar and meat the moment back then. I often doubt my ability to do it now, but I am definitely getting better.

And so my desire for my children is the same. Of course, like my parents, I still barge into their lives, play time and personal space asking, "Hey! What's going on in here?" I still throw broad and general concepts their way. I hesitate to connect every dot in every moment with the hope that they are learning transferable skills and connecting the dots themselves. But I don't let them dangle from the cliff of correction for too long. I give them room to explore, adapt and adjust their behavior to the moment and expectations created by the environment, but not to unrepairable detriment. And if all goes according to plan, they will barge into their own lives and the lives of people around them asking often and deeply, "Hey, what's going on in here?"

List some ways in which you use accountability.

_____

_____

_____

_____

_____

_____

_____

_____

_____

_____

_____

_____

_____

_____

_____

_____

LIST 11: HOLDING HANDS

(February 26, 2016)

A few funny things I've seen in the last few days....

---

1. A lady perk up her breast while sitting in her car at a stop light.
2. **A man cursing out a woman at 711 while holding hands with his daughter.**
3. A man sharing a latte with his dog.
4. An older man holding his bottom while running to the bathroom at the movies.
5. A guy try to spit out of his car window...but the window was up.
6. A toddler playing with his mom's nipple...at the mall...in the food court...and she didn't stop the kid. LOL!
7. An old man spike his friends drink...at a golf course...before heading out to their tee-time. LOL!!

James Powell III – "I gotta start hanging out with you!!!!"

Cassi Mitzs – "#4 I actually laughed out loud"

Katrina McCaslin – "HOW do you catch all these things!!!"

Kristi Clingenpeel Maxwell – "You've had an interesting week my friend!!!! #4 is the best!!!"

Jeannie McMahan – "Dude, there is nothing you won't write about, and the morning people won't DO?! Hahaha"

E.J. Johnson – "smh, we are an entertaining species"

Rebecca Simcoe – "You make my day! Thank you."

Joshua Pease – "These are the best updates!"

Donny Chastain – "I wanna hang out half a day with you and take notes. We will prolly laugh the whole time. Especially on the golf course. Now that's funny stuff there. [...]"

Mandy Maberry – "I think my life would be more fun if I rode with you!"

THE STORY

I pulled up to Seven Eleven to get some gas and a coffee (no judgement for Seven Eleven Columbian Roast…it hits the spot when I'm on the road). After pumping my gas, locking the cap and holstering the gun, I leave my car and approach the store. Only a few steps away from making it into the store, I hear a bit of commotion behind me. I turn to see two cars stalemated at a gas pump. From what I can gather, one car pulled past the pump and was attempting to back in. At the same time, the other car pulled into the pump the other car was preparing to back into. The backing car honked. The car that pulled in parked, the driver got out and began to pump gas.

At this point, the car that was attempting to back into the spot, speeds around to another pump on the other side and parks. He gets out of the car and immediately starts to yell and curse at the other car that took "his spot". (By now, I have identified the two drivers. The car that pulled into the pump appeared to be a woman in her mid-30s, professionally dressed. The driver of the other car appeared to be a male in his mid-40s, soccer dad-ish.) As he's yelling and cursing, he walks to the other side of his car, opens the rear passenger door, reaches in and pulls out a female child who appears to be six or seven years old. I assume she was his daughter.

As he pulls his daughter out of the car and closes the door, he continues to curse and yell. He walks toward the other car while holding his daughter's hand and continues to curse and yell. (I mean...I can only think of a few times I've ever heard someone use this kind of language toward another person in the presence of children. This, by far, was the worse one.) Eventually, the guy and his daughter walk away from the car, into the store and then come back to their car. This time his daughter has a donut and juice in one hand and her dad's hand in the other. As he is approaching his car, he continues to yell and curse while putting his daughter back into the car. He buckles her in, closes the door, goes back to the other side of his car and begins to pump his gas while still cursing and yelling at the lady who took "his spot". Finally, the lady finishes pumping her gas, locks the cap and holsters the gun. I thought she was going to get in her car and drive away because of all of the commotion, but she locks her car and heads toward the store. As she's walking toward the store, the guy is still at the pump cursing and yelling.

I know you're thinking, "Derrick, why are you standing outside watching all of this?!" Because I'm nosey, OKAY! I admit it.

As the lady is walking from her car to the store, she has to pass me to walk through the doors. I made eye contact with her and said, "Man, that guy is having a rough morning, huh?" She replied, "Yeah, I cut him off about a mile ago and accidentally stole his pump. I get him being angry, but he's got something else going on. If he's all yelled out by the time I get back out there, I'll try to apologize." Sure enough, she grabbed a coffee, walked out of the store and directly to his car. I couldn't hear what they said, but his demeanor completely changed as she continually pointed to the back seat where his daughter sat. A few moments later, they shook hands, parted ways and drove off in their individual cars.

I watched in amazement. Then went inside to buy my coffee.

THE OBSERVATION

I saw a guy who was obviously upset at one moment (the lady cut him off in traffic) which turned into another moment (the lady stole his pump) which snowballed into a full-fledged fit. Not only did it turn into a full-fledged fit, but he did it in front of his daughter and all of the on-lookers that were either pumping their gas or purchasing something in the store. He didn't care who saw or who heard, including his daughter.

It made me ask questions like, "Is this a normal response for him?" "I wonder if something happened before the other lady cut him off in traffic?" While I don't have answers to any of those questions, I couldn't help but turn my outward and external thoughts inward. Have I done something like that before? Was it at home in front of my family and friends? Have I responded like this in a more public place? What would cause me to respond in such a way? What could I do to control and prevent a similar response?

As I write this, I remember my son playing a soccer game against a rival team. One of the players from the other team picked my son up and slammed him to the ground...in a soccer game! I wasn't there, but was being told the story by my wife, my son and a parent from our team. I vividly remember texting the other parent from our team saying, "Stuff like this makes me want to fight the dad of the player and spit in the mom's face." WHAT?! Did I really text that to another parent? Yes. Did I really think that?! Yes. Did I really admit to that thought and put it in this book?! Yes.

While I was looking at the guy from Seven Eleven have a complete meltdown in front of his daughter, it could have easily been me at my son's soccer game....in front of my son family, teammates and his friends.

THE LESSON

I wonder how often people get so caught up in the moment, they forget where they are and who is around them? I know I've done that before. In fact, I believe many of us have done it before. It may not have been at a gas pump or a soccer game, but it may have been in the privacy of your own home. OR a movie theater with a talking patron. OR a parking lot with something who took a parking spot. OR a teacher who presumptuously mistreated your child. OR with your neighbor who refuses to bring their trashcan back into their yard after trash day or who fails to keep their yard trimmed.

OR…fill in the blank. Heck, I can't come up with all of the scenarios. BUT insert your scenario and misbehavior…and this story could easily be about you.

Every one of us has a moment where we lose our cool or act out of character. It is in those moments we learn to humble ourselves and extend grace to others. We can relate because of our personal experience with our errors. Don't be so quick to judge or cast judgement. Don't be so quick to cut ties or penalize character. Don't be so harsh in your decision making. Because in the same way that I saw a man curse out a women while holding his daughter's hand, is the same way….. insert my story…..insert your story.

List some times you've been an example by holding it together and keeping your cool.

_____

_____

_____

_____

_____

_____

_____

_____

_____

_____

_____

_____

_____

_____

LIST 12: LAUGHING

(February 20, 2016)

Today....in the park, I saw people....

1. Kissing
2. **Laughing**
3. Cooking
4. Playing
5. Practicing
6. Exercising
7. Praying
8. Working
9. Holding Hands
10. Loving

I saw fathers and sons, mothers and daughters, coaches and athletes, black folks and white folks...enjoying life together. I saw people enjoying the company of others, enjoying the earth and the sun that warms it, being rejuvenated by laughter and love. And it didn't feel awkward. In fact, it felt right. As it should.

Shaunteia Powell – "I am so happy you came and played with us!!!!"

Johnathan Powell – "It was an awesome time. We will be doing a lot more of this soon."

Tiffany Whisman – "I saw the same."

Ashley Semone – "Jeez Derrick that was beautiful! Makes me excited for spring!"

THE STORY

I'm a people watcher. I watch people. For absolutely no reason at all, at any time during the day or week, in any scenario, I find myself looking at people....looking for a story, a reason to hope and love and believe. This time, I found hope, love and belief in a park.

Sometimes, when my wife has the kids and I have a gap in my schedule, I find a park. In that park, I find a path. Eventually, that path leads me to a sitting place. This time, that sitting place was a bench. This time, there was no one on the bench, so I sat. I sat on the right edge of the bench with the hope that someone would come along and ask to sit there with me....because I'm a talker and love to meet new people. Unfortunately, no one did such a thing. I think it was because it was such a great day for walking.

Since I was by myself and all of the passer-byes were either preoccupied by their walking goals or walking with someone, I began to take notice of everyone that passed me. Thin. Round. Short. Tall. Black. White. Asian. Couple. Single. Mother. Father. Child. Fast. Slow. Sweaty. Jeans. Yoga pants. Eye contact and smile. Super focused and ignored me. Casual walker. Exercise walker. Talker walker. Stop-and-stretch-because-I'm-done walker. Scenic walker. Meditator/prayer. Mom walking with kids. Hand-holder walkers. Happy walkers. I-hate-doing-this-but-I-like-how-my-pants-fit-after-I-do walker. Serious walker. And, ironically, laughing walkers. Laughing? How could someone laugh and walk? Laugh and exercise? There's nothing humorous about exercise OR walking. Those were the things that stuck out to me the most. But why?

THE OBSERVATION

At some point in my life, I think I've been every single kind of these walkers. Maybe not the white or Asian walker...or the mother walker....but you get what I'm saying. Depending on what life has dealt me that day, I could be any of these walkers. However, I don't think I've ever been the laughing walker. And I'm a funny guy. I make jokes. I find humor in everything....besides exercise. Does that mean there is an area of life that my humor doesn't touch. How is that? I should have more control than that.

I was leaving one of my son's soccer tournaments. It was after a tough game in which we lost 2-1. It was against a team we should have beat, but we were missing players, our boys were just plain ol' dog tired and there was some questionable officiating (of course). As we walked to the car, we noticed there were a lot of other parents leaving the game, as expected. This means the exit would be rather crowded. We squeezed through the walking traffic, got into our car and began to attempt to pull into traffic. Out of nowhere, Craig Groeschel, the senior pastor of one of the largest churches in America, comes jogging away from the soccer field and towards his car. Before he gets into his car, he scans the traffic, a smirk creeps onto his face, he shakes his head, laughs and gets into his car. As he begins to pull out, he rolls down his window, makes eye contact with the car across from him, gives the friendly wave, is allowed access, exits his parking space and pulls out into traffic. Eventually, he leaves the complex and on to wherever he was headed.

Now, that day, for whatever reason, there were some angry soccer moms and dads driving some pretty big minivans and SUVs. They could have been angry because of poor officiating, their team's loss or the terrible traffic exiting the complex. For whichever reason, they were taking it out on each other and all of the bystanders by honking their horns and gesturing very vividly out of their windows. And out of nowhere, here comes a guy with a big smile and friendly wave softening the atmosphere with a gentle merge. Having seen so, I imitated the same gesture and was also allowed access, even though my son's loss, poor officiating and crowded parking lot suggested my response should be differently.

THE LESSON

We never know who is watching us. In the same way I sat in that park on that bench and watched all of those different people…in the same way I saw Pastor Craig Groeschel laugh at a presumably tough situation …is the same way someone may be looking at me.

Pastor Craig will probably never read this book, but with that simple gesture, he has forever changed the way I leave soccer games. LOL! Seriously. And even though I may not expect it, someone may be watching me. They could have been watching me exit the game that day. OR exit traffic after the game. People could possibly be watching the way I treat my wife or interact with my children. They could be watching my dietary choices or community activism. They could be watching my social behavior or professional partnerships. What they observe could possible forever change the way they see black people or men or fathers or husbands or soccer dads or…..whatever.

What should my response be?! In every situation, it should be to observe, resolve, laugh at it confidently and act. I can't change every situation. I can change my response to it and possibly even… laugh at it.

List some ways your positive perspective has changed a potentially negative outcome.

_____

_____

_____

_____

_____

_____

_____

_____

_____

_____

_____

_____

_____

_____

LIST 13: FREESTYLE

(February 11, 2016)

A few things my wife does for me that I take for granted....

1. Keeps veggies on my plate.
2. Mediates all conflict in the house.
3. Knows all things Sier kids related.
4. Tells me the truth, especially when I don't want to hear it.
5. Let's me chase my dreams.
6. Forgives me daily.
7. Rotates my drying and bathing towels.
8. Flips the toilet paper when I face it the "wrong" way. (It does work better, I admit.)
9. Loves 270 lb Derrick just the same as, if not more, than 180 lb Derrick.
10. Buys my clothes. I refuse to shop.
11. Changes out my toothbrush.
12. When I'm stressed, she rubs my head until I fall asleep.
13. Keeps my feet looking handsome.
14. **Let's me freestyle to her over the phone while she's at work, even though I know she has stuff to do and maybe sometimes regrets she answered the phone.**
15. Sits thru Star Trek when she really wants to catch up on Dexter.

I see you, babe! And I appreciate you.

For all the ladies, keep it up! We could do it without you, we just wouldn't live as long...and life wouldn't be nearly as fun or fulfilling. Fellas, acknowledgement and a simple thank you goes a looooong way.

Reggie Pratcher – "Voicemail because your voice smells freestyle is a classic."

Lashonda Malrey-Horne – "So sweet! Glad you know how lucky you are. I expect something like 'stays fine for me.' Lol"

Jyntel L. Tipton – "I love this Sier!!!!"

Christi Perrin – "Saaawweeeet way to start the Valentine's Day weekend DUDE!! BOOM! ;-) On the serious note however… isn't your WIFE GRAND! Amen and amen!! Blessings to you and yours Sir!"

Lindsay Hale Parke – "This is a great idea. I love the appreciation of your spouse."

LaTonya Harrison Porter – "Award Winning post!!"

Sybil Burrell – "We need more Derrick Sier's of the world. It sure would be a better place."

Gina Michelle Henson Marshall – "What a great compliment!! Well said."

Jessica Wagner – "D, so very sweet! She's amazing and it's nice to see a man celebrate his wife! ~j"

THE STORY

My wife is a busy lady; probably more busy than I'd like her to be. And that's not me trying to control her schedule or actions. I know she does a lot of things she doesn't want to do, but she does them for the sake of the family….or to keep the peace at her job. Either way, I know she would much prefer to spend her time doing other more productive and leisurely things.

Well, sometimes, I take it upon myself to be her break from the more mature things of life by calling her at work and rapping to her over the phone. Now, honestly, I'm not the best rapper in the world. I know you were thinking otherwise, but rapping is probably one of the things I'm the worst at doing. Seriously. It's pretty bad. With this is mind, it's really hard for her to listen to me rap, unplanned and unwritten, smack-dab in the middle of the busiest part of her work day.

I might call and start out with, "Uh…you know what time it is." And she's like, "Derrick. No." And I'm like, "Yeah girl, I'm about to rap for you. Keep it clean like Dove for you." And she's like, "Derrick. Please. No." At this point, she has the option and freedom, without judgement or repercussion, to hang up and text me at her leisure, but 99% of the time, she will stay on the phone and wait until I run out of rhyming words. Keep in mind, during this entire freestyle, I could be talking about food, the weather, basketball or whatever words fit my rhyme scheme. Sure, I'll bring it back around to her somehow, but the rhyming takes precedence.

The entire time, she's showing tremendous patience and displaying an immense amount of grace.

THE OBSERVATION

There are two main thoughts I take away from this reflection. The first, I absolutely love it when my wife answers my calls in the middle of the day. I understand it's a crap shoot if she'll be able to answer them anyways, but I try. Most of the time, I get a voicemail and leave the rap on the voicemail. But every now and again, she answers and I get to hear her voice….and she gets to hear mine. Ha! And that absolutely makes my day.

The second, I know she loves it when I call her. You know how I know? She tells me she does. When my name and number pops up on her phone, she never knows what the situation could be. Very few times is it something serious. Most of the time, it's me just wanting to check on her, hear about her day or just spit some rhymes. And as frustrated as she gets when I call for absolutely nothing besides to freestyle to her, she secretly loves it. How do I know that? She told me.

THE LESSON

Connecting with people can never be built on the sporadic, inconsistent and rare big things. True, those moments stand out and create a lasting crater in the memory of the receiver. But true relationship, true rapport and true depth comes from the consistent, small, significant, thoughtful, intentional and unique connections made over time.

It reminds me of the kid who lived with his mother and received visits from his father. The mother handled the brunt of the day to day work; homework, studying, lunches, sports practices, bedtime, showers, discipline, fruits and veggies, limited TV and technology, grandparent visits, etc. The father came along with big gifts, high energy, lax rules and junk food visits. One day, the boy was notified that because of his excellent grades, he and other students were taking a trip to an amusement park and could only bring one parent. The mother thought, surely, the boy would choose his father, but the son chose his mother. When she asked him why, he said, "Mom, you're the reason I have good grades. Dad is the reason I have cavities."

I'm sure my wife gets tens of calls throughout the day. Bill collectors. Friends. Random community contacts. But she only answers one call. Mine. Even though she knows she's going to get a pointless freestyle that is going to knock her socks off and make her day, she answers it anyway.

Everyone should have someone answering their calls. And everyone should have someone to whom they can call and freestyle.

List some unique ways in which you connect with people.

Captain's Log. Star Date 21176.455

Lieutenant Commander Ethan's fascination with my stomach has continued to grow. During snuggle time, I found him measuring the depth of my belly button with his pinky finger. He will slap it open-hand and then count how long it jiggles in seconds. He likes to listen to it growl and then try to guess what I ate for lunch. He is convinced, if I was a villain or super hero, my stomach would be my super power. I will conduct further research with the hopes of curbing and/or appeasing his curiosity. Number One has ruled out corporal punishment [for Lieutenant Commander] and recommended exercise [for me] instead. We will continue to search for alternative options.

THE STORY

When I was younger, my dad and I were huge snugglers. It wasn't a traditional snuggle because my dad is too much of a man's man for that. However, he would lay down on his side while watching TV and I would lay on his side, just to be close. I loved spending time like this with my dad so much, that at an early age, I determined my son and I would do the same thing.

Well, here I am 15 years later with a similar snuggle opportunity of my own. Of course, I'm not the manly man my dad was, so I'm like, "Bring it in, son!" I'm laying shirtless on my back and inviting him to choose an arm pit in which to snuggle. Once he chooses, he lays his ear on my chest and places his hand on my belly. Without fail, his pinky always finds a way to my belly button and that becomes the focus of his nine-year-old fidget while watching TV. After he gets bored with the belly button, he then begins his slight fascination with the jiggle of my 270 pound frame. This is the bane of our snuggle time.

THE OBSERVATION

I love that that my son is so affectionate. Just as equally, I love his curiosity and willingness to explore. He asks questions which catch me off guard and provides simple and effective answers to those questions, implying he thought about them before asking, my stomach not excluded.

After I noticed my belly button became the focus of his fidget, I asked him, "What's up with you and my belly button?" He asked, "Why did you let it get so deep?" This lead to a conversation about health, exercise, food choices and the results from the combination of those things. A level of accountability came out of that conversation which I could have never predicted. In fact, after that, he resolved to have a fruit and/or vegetable at every meal and if he spent too much time in the house or in front of electronics, he would let everyone in the house know it was about time for some outside time.

His curiosity has impacted our entire family.

THE LESSON

As parents, we should take advantage of every opportunity to explore and develop the minds of our little ones. We should be their primary and most influential impact. They should be shaped and molded by the wisdom resting in our hearts, minds and souls. We should eagerly share what we know and admit when we don't know. We should lead and guide, then be ready to switch to come alongside, support, cheer and coach while they take lead. Why? Because they have an entire world competing for their attention with information in hand, ready to feed any open mind through microaggressions and subliminal messaging. Sure, some of the information may be good, but some of it may be bad. It is up to us to do our best, set them up for the best and hope they are able to make some sense out of the mess.

You say you don't have kids? One of my best friends is just now settling into her own skin. It's beautiful to watch it happen up close. At 36 years young, she is discovering who she is, what she wants to do, how she wants to do it and where it will take her when done correctly. And the same way I find compersion in seeing my son discover life for himself is the same joy I feel watching my friend discover herself in her own way.

This concept of discovery happens in every aspect of life. Where there is a person snuggling up close to an idea or concept, purpose or passion; they are close to discovery. All it takes is a little courage to question and discomfort to search....and you too will find yourself measuring the belly button of your dream, wondering why it's so deep or in many cases, so shallow.

List some exciting things you've recently discovered about yourself.

_____

_____

_____

_____

_____

_____

_____

_____

_____

_____

_____

_____

_____

_____

_____

_____

LIST 15: FOCUS

(January 22, 2016)

I talk to my son all the time about focusing. Focus on what's important. Finish what you started. Commit to giving your best. Never give up. The hope is that it will resonate and stick... and he'll be known for these three things: stamina, grit and being a man of his word.

If we get our boys to **focus on what's important instead of on what's popular**, they'll become the men we all know they can be.

#FDMoon #TieDay #MenINTraining #Mentor4LIFE

Chrisinda Gonzalez – "Derrick, you are incredible!!!! Just wanted you to know."

Tequia Sier – "Dad to many...starting with mine. Thanks!"

Heather McFarland – "You're all sorts of amazingness!"

THE STORY

My friends, Taylor Doe and Warren Pete, have committed their life to working within their local community. Not only their local community, but also working with children within that community. Not only working with children within that community, but also working with the young men within that community. This passion has lead them to start an event called Tie Day. Tie Day is all about connecting young men with older men and also serving them by exampling healthy life skills, responsibility, confidence and managing the perception of others via fashion.....hence, the ties.

The way the event goes is Taylor and Warren partner with several people and organizations within the community. These partners then reach out to their connections with the hope of generating enough interest, people/mentors and collecting enough ties for every single young man in the targeted school. Once mentors have been solidified, interest has been stirred and ties have been collected, community leaders are contacted, social media is mobilized, and media outlets are notified of the greatness that's about to take place.

Regarding the actual event, speakers are invited and given several minutes to talk about healthy life skills, being a responsible young man, the importance of confidence and managing the perception of others via their wardrobe. After the speakers have set the tone, mentors are paired with students, ties are distributed, the mentors and mentees spend time together talking about those major concepts and learning/teaching how to knot ties. It's a very powerful event, even if for the visual alone.

THE OBSERVATION

We are always amazed at a few things: 1) How many young men either don't own a tie, 2) How many don't know how to knot a tie, 3) How many mentors are willing to give up their day to impart into these young men and 4) The amount of impact that is created by partnering mentors and mentees together, even if for a few hours. It means, something as simple as a Tie Day can go a long way as it pertains to the impact it has on the community.

When I was younger, my dad was deep into suits and ties. So, knotting a tie was something I learned at a very early age. I was probably 8 years old when I learned to knot a tie. However, this means someone who knew how to knot a tie was around in my life to show me how to do it. Which means someone was around, available and willing to show me. Which means someone was personally invested in my knowing how to knot a tie. Which means someone found value in passing on knowledge so I could be a better person.

Tie Day, while simply revolving around people and ties, has a deeper meaning. It has to do with a group of people, possessing a certain amount of wisdom and knowledge, passing that information on to the next generation. This information comes through personal contact and exampling. And as with my father, some of our greatest Tie Day interactions come while showing these young men how to knot a tie.

THE LESSON

Organizations want to create and implement these huge initiatives to reach these unreached groups. Soup kitchens. Clothing closets. Housing units. Medical tents. Government aid. While all of these efforts meet a need, the greatest need one could ever meet is that of time, information and empowerment. Soup kitchens only exist because people are hungry. Clothing closets only exist because people don't have clothing. Housing units, the same. Medical tents, the same. Government aid, the same.

My dream is that we begin to take time and empower people with the means and knowledge to acquire all of those things for themselves instead of them relying on someone else to provide it for them. I believe this process can start with something as simple as a tie. How? I'm not only going to give them a tie, but I'm going to show them how to knot it. I'm not only going to show them how to knot it, but I'm going to show them the outfit with which they wear the tie. Not only am I going to identify the outfit, but I'm going to tell them where and why they wear the outfit which is topped off with an appropriate tie which has a killer knot. And I'll help them learn and acquire the skill for the job/interview at which they will wear that outfit and tie with the killer knot. And I'll explain, if they look and dress the part, and actually get the part, and do the part well, then they can feed themselves, dress themselves, purchase their own homes and make sure they have the benefits to monitor their health and the health of their family....all beginning with the gift and conversation revolving around a tie and a knot.

It's more than a tie. It's more than a knot. It's about

connecting people and passing information. It's about exampling. Forget what's popular in the moment. It's about refocusing on what's important for the future. In this case, a tie.

List some future goals you are currently preparing for now.

_____

_____

_____

_____

_____

_____

_____

_____

_____

_____

_____

_____

_____

_____

LIST 16: THE EXTRA MILE

(January 21, 2016)

Just saw a lady run out of her garage to give her man a kiss and ran back inside. Well...it's freakin cold outside! And she was underdressed and barefoot. Respect. Here's why...

1. **Going the extra mile sometimes is only a few feet.**
2. He had a huge smile on his face.
3. The last thing they did before they parted ways was... connect.
4. She sacrifice her comfort inside to come out into the cold where he was.
5. It's the small things that make great relationships.

Just my thoughts....

Chris Cole Williams – "Good stuff brother!!!"

Heather McFarland – "Love this post! These points are SPOT ON!"

Bill Moyers – "if all couples did things like this for each other there would be far less divorce"

Robin Summers Gonzalez – "Amen brother. AMEN!!"

Brie A. Reynolds – "'Going the extra mile sometimes is only a few feet.' Love this!"

Kristin Jacoway Fitzgerald – "I kind of consider you my FB Life Coach. Our first point is SPOT ON & something I needed to hear today."

Paul Geisinger – "Couldn't have said it better myself! Great words brother!!

THE STORY

My wife and I have lived in this neighborhood for a few years now. We live on a dead end street next to two of the longest tenants of the neighborhood. Both tenants have lived there for over 35 years. In fact, one of the tenants is the one who attempted to help me with my lawnmower (List 6). We have a feel for what goes on, who does what, when they do it, how they do it, what's acceptable and what's not acceptable. This means that, for the most part, everyone does everything the same way. We know what time people go to work. When their children go to school. When everyone gets home. Who visits on the weekend. What time the mail runs and the trash pick-ups are. When I tell you everything is predictable and regimented, it is.

So, one day, I decided to break the mold, leave early and take a different route out of the neighborhood. Where I would normally leave our dead-end street and take a right, this day, I took a left. As soon as I did, I noticed a garage slowly raise and open. Our comes a well-suited man with a trash bag in one hand and a briefcase in the other. Once he tossed the trash bag in the can on the side of the house, he headed toward his car. He opened the rear driver's side door first, threw his briefcase in, shut the rear driver's side door and as he went to reach for the front driver's side door, this underdressed barefoot lady comes shuffling out of the open, still-raised garage door and toward the man still standing outside of the car. She came around the car, kissed the man dead-square on his lips, smiled, turned and shuffled back into the house. The garage lowered and closed, the man got in the car, started it, back out and as he passed me going out of the neighborhood, I could see the huge smile on this face.

THE OBSERVATION

Let me start out by saying it was cold. I'm not talking about that early morning summer cold. I'm talking about that

February in Oklahoma, it's approaching spring, but it's still winter morning cold. Like….if you close your eyes, you might think it's December kind of cold. The man was obviously trying to get rid of the trash and get in his car as soon as possible. While he was dressed for the weather, he was dressed for house-to-the-car weather which is different than let-me-stand-outside-weather. I can only imagine what he thought when he had to wait for his wife to come all the way out of the house to his car. I can also only imagine what he thought when he saw that she was barely dressed AND barefoot.

On the other side, I can only imagine what kind of courage she had to build up to know what the weather was like compared to what she was wearing and still come outside to kiss her husband. There are a lot of factors at play. Regardless of the temporary inconvenience, they were able to connect and both of their days were distinctly changed because of it. At least that's what happened in my head.

THE LESSON

I was at the school walking with one of my mentees. As we were walking down the hallway, we passed a piece of trash. I asked him to pick up that piece of trash. He responded, "Don't they pay people to do that? Besides, if I picked up all of the trash I passed, I would be out here all day." I replied, "They do have people to clean up the trash. And I didn't ask you to pick up all of the trash. I asked you to pick up THAT piece of trash." He had a little attitude, but he picked it up anyway. As a result, one of the teachers saw his actions, highlighted his gesture in front of his classmates and he was rewarded with a trip to the café. I don't know if he ever did it again, but he did it that day.

I took that same route from my house and through the neighborhood several more times. I never saw that couple repeat the morning exchange again. I don't know if that was a one-time exchange. I don't know if he headed in to work early that day and that was the only reason I caught them locking lips. I don't know if that is something they do all of the time or never again. I do know…they did it once….and I got a chance to see it.

I told my wife about it and how much it impressed me. Soon, she started intentionally kissing me before I left the house. Don't get us wrong, we normally kiss before leaving each other's presence, but she made it a point to make our final exchange before leaving the house...a kiss. A simple gesture that, over the years, has gone a long way.

Sometimes, when we think about making life changing decisions, we are paralyzed or frozen by the massiveness of that decision. However, every marathon begins with a single step. Every mountain is scaled one foot a time. Every cake is baked one minute at a time. You catch my drift? Smell what I'm cooking?

Are you trying to repair a relationship? It can start with a phone call, text or apology. Are you trying to break some bad habits? Start by not doing it just one time. Trying to lose weight? It can start with one workout or one meal. Trying to save for a big purchase or payoff? It starts with one dollar. Chasing a dream? Write it out. Want to start or finish a degree? Take one class. Want to be promoted at your job? Come early. Stay late. Let your supervisor know you're interested. Want to make friends? Show yourself friendly. Want to plant a garden? Start with a pot of tomatoes. Whatever it is. No matter the size. Whether it's doing what's required or going above and beyond, it starts with one action – one step toward that goal.

List some life-long areas in which you need to start taking simple steps today.

_____

_____

_____

_____

_____

_____

_____

_____

_____

_____

_____

_____

_____

_____

LIST 17: HUG MORE OFTEN

(January 18, 2016)

I wanna give out 100 hugs today at the parade. If you see me... come squeeze my neck!

I only got 78. So, project #100MLKhugs was a fail.

It was fun trying tho. I hugged...

1. 11 people I didn't know. Both were group hugs already taking place.
2. 13 parents of kids I've worked with.
3. 18 people before the parade even started.
4. Just as many men as women.
5. Just as many kids as adults.
6. A few people who I knew weren't huggers, but I was trying to get to 100.
7. A lady whose mouth almost touched mine.
8. **Three people who I should definitely hug more often.**
9. Donald Woody Sr. His church was deep today!
10. John Pettis. His squad was also deep!

Bonus: I saw J. Wiggins, but he was with his people. I'll bro him up next time.

Latoya Monique – "its okay you never know til you try... LOL...next year at the end go up to the school bands and hug them im sure you get the last 22"

Terri L Dobyns-Brockman – "You are such an inspiration Derrick!"

THE STORY

My kids have attended Camp Shiloh for several years now. Camp Shiloh is a not-for-profit non-residential camp targeting inner city kids during the summer break. They provide a top-notch faith-based outdoor experience for kids who probably wouldn't otherwise get the opportunity to do so. In addition to serving their community in a unique way, they give their community partners an opportunity to partner with and serve the same community in an as equally impressive way through food and volunteers.

I've known several of the seasonal staff, full-time staff and operating crew for Shiloh for quite some time. Our social and community circles had begun to cross even more so and it was only a matter of time before my family had the opportunity to partner with them outside of the summer camp experience. Coincidentally, Camp Shiloh sent out an email inviting their community partners and campers to participate on their Martin Luther King Jr. parade day float. My kids and I jumped at the opportunity.

Of course, I couldn't just sit on the float and wave at people. In addition to passing out information about the upcoming summer camp, I made a personal goal to hug 100 people at the parade. Why? I'm a hugger and it gave me an extra incentive to connect.

THE OBSERVATION

Initially, it was easy to get hugs because I was around people I knew. People on the float. Camp Shiloh workers or campers. Later on, because I'm fairly active in the community, I would see some of the kids and their family from the schools at which I volunteered and worked. After that, I was in full-fledged hug mode.

In the process of failing my goal of 100 hugs, I noticed a few things about people. There are three basic hug groups. 1) People who love hugs. 2) People who hate hugs. 3) People who are indifferent to hugs and probably wouldn't hug at all, but they will hug if they come across someone who is as big of a hugger as I am. The third group of people are the most common and the most hilarious!

I mean, I was coming in hard with the open hug arms. I ignored all of the traditional social clues like the extended fist for fist bumps and open palms for hand-shakes. I ignored the full body lean away. I ignored the non-eye contact. I ignored the turn away. I'm telling you, I blew through all of the stop signs in an attempt to get my 100 hugs. Even at that, I feel significantly short, but I did get 78 hugs.

THE LESSON

There are various levels of social interaction; hugging being one, but obviously, not the most popular and probably, aside from kissing (popular in non-American cultures), the most invasive. However, this doesn't mean that people aren't open to social interaction. Most people just prefer it to take place on their own terms. People tend to think everyone should interact according to their preference. However, there's always a happy medium that can be reached.

I'm a hugger. A pretty intense hugger, in fact. Toe to toe, chest to chest, touching belly buttons, cheek to cheek, arms around your back…good ol' hugger. This is my preferred form of greeting. I would have very few friends if I made everyone comply to my preferred form of greeting. Additionally, I would be equally frustrated if people started avoiding me because they thought I was going to bully them into hugging every time we connected. And because I enjoy a milder variation of greeting in a hand-shake, fist pound or side-hug rather than having no greeting at all, I comply. I try really hard to not allow my zeal and preference to overtake the comfort of the person I encounter.

Everyone doesn't take this approach. For many, it's their way or the highway. And I'm not just talking about hugs. I'm sure you've come across someone like this at your job, on the PTA, a coach, teacher, neighbor, family member, romantic partner, community or religious leader, politician….many of you probably have friends like this.

And so the question becomes: who sets their preference

aside for the sake of interaction? If I'm a hugger and the other person is not, do I become a hand-shaker or do they become a hugger? Do we find some hybrid of the two where we shake with one hand and simultaneously hug with the other? Do we let the loud parent dominate the PTA meeting because they "get stuff done"? When and how do we get the ideas of everyone else in the room heard? Do we let the mean coach continue to be mean because that's the way he coaches? What about the other players that don't respond to yelling and hitting? Do we allow the musical theater teacher to mishandle the student actors because we fear that saying something will jeopardize our participating child's odds at getting a part in upcoming productions? Do we allow injustices to continue to take place with the fear of also becoming a target? Do direct reports continue to adjust to leadership styles instead of leadership adjusting to their employee's workstyles? Who gives? Should it not go both ways?

For me, there is always the fear of…if I continue to comply, I'll become someone I'm not. And as a hugger, one of my greatest fears is being stuck in a room full of hand-shakers. Sure, I can comply for a while, but eventually, either somebody is getting a hug or I'm going to have to find a different group! The same goes for jobs, friends, social groups, communities, etc. I'll stay for a while, but eventually, something has to give.

While at the parade, I started out on a hot streak. The hugs kept me plugged in. Over time, the hugs got fewer and fewer…meaning, the parade, for me, became less and less fun. I became more disengaged. I lost my fever. I wonder how this plays in other areas of my life? Friends? Goals? Community involvement? Family? Faith? Do I disengage in those areas when things aren't going my way? OR do I adjust? However it works out, I know it's good for me to have at least a few "huggers" in those areas of my life to keep me engaged. If not, my compromise/adjustment turns bitter and the parade of life is no longer fun. I know that about myself. What are those areas of your life? How do adjust or compromise? Are you hugging those areas of you life more often? OR have you disengaged?

List a few people and/or things that serve as a source of encouragement.

_____

_____

_____

_____

_____

_____

_____

_____

_____

_____

_____

_____

_____

LIST 18: BOOTYQUAKES

(January 6, 2016)

10 Different ways my kids describe «passing gas»:

1. Poot
2. Booty Burp
3. Dookie Dust
4. **Bootyquakes**
5. Farting
6. Gasatosis
7. Booty Clap
8. Crop Dusting
9. Butt Whistle
10. Canadian Hello

LOL! I love these kids.

Nailah J. Pennington – "LOL My kids found this hilarious"

Joshua Pease – "Canadian Hello is new!"

Mark Johnson – "What a gas!"

Monica Stephens – "So now we know where they get their sense of humor!"

Ceanti' Aldridge – "Dookie dust??!!!!! Haaaaa!!!!"

LaToya L. Davis-Mason – "I could hang with your kids"

Ashley Rhodes – "Dookie dust has my side hurting from laughing!!!!!!!!!!!"

Nikki Young – "BHAHAHAHAHAHA! "Dookie Dust" tho?!?! Yeah, those are DEFINITELY your kids!!!!"

THE STORY

I'm not sure if every two-parent family has polar parenting; meaning, one parent is all business and the other parent has the responsibility to be fun. If that's the model, our family has it down packed. If it's not normal, we are anomalies. My wife is very much so the calendar keeper, bill payer, shot record holder...type of lady. I am the "let's have cereal for dinner" parent. I'm not saying one is better or more important than the other, but no kid has ever said, "You remember that one time mom made us do our homework?!" Ha!

Well, one of the things mom doesn't like is potty-humor. Anything having to do with making fun of using the restroom, mom steers the kids…..and dad….away from. I'm not sure what she thinks is going to happen if we talk about it for an extended period of time. Does she think we are going to come up with clever names for them and those names are going to be repeated and possibly put on social media for the world to see or maybe in a book for the world to read?! Since none of that is plausible, this just means we get to talk about it that much more when mom isn't around. That's exactly what happens.

Hence the list.

THE OBSERVATION

My kids deserve way more credit for their creativity than I give them. Matter of fact, this list was so creative, after we finished this list, I started asking them about nicknames for other things. What do you call this? What do you call that? Where did that come from? I was surprised they were so eager to share some of those things. No way would I have shared stuff like this with my parents. But then I started to ask myself, "Are they generally this open with all adults or just me?" I know what I wanted my answer to be, but I couldn't be sure, so I had to poll the other adults I knew they interacted with significantly.

"Hey, what are the kids talking about when they are over your house?" "Hey, when the kids are in the car with you, are they talking about anything? Not even this?"

I found that many of the other adults in their lives weren't giving them the opportunity to be as expressive or the freedom to act freely and think unfiltered and out loud...not even at school. So many of the adults around them were telling them how and what to think instead of asking them what they were thinking or why they thought that way. So, when I opened the door to expressiveness, whether it be silly or meaningless, it opened the door of rapport to have other conversations.

Since this approach went over so well, I tried it with my godchildren, my mentee group, kids at the church and students at the schools at which I worked. The results were all the same. Build rapport. Communicate on their level. Give them room and space to be themselves. Provoke them with progressively inquisitive topics and respond with even lower judgement. Watch how quickly they open up. Watch how much you learn about their lives and the way they see the world.

Oh yeah, this works with almost everyone. Not just children. Show interest. Be genuine. Ask questions. Reserve judgement. Voila.

THE LESSON

Maybe everyone wants to share a piece of their story. They are just waiting for the right people to come along with the tender touch of friendship. For me and my children, it took us joking over things we could name our farts. I didn't have to take off my adult hat to do so. I didn't have to take off my dad hat to do so. I honestly believe they want to share with me the cool and scary and confusing and challenging things in their lives. They just needed the time and space; they needed to be provoked and not judged.

I wonder how many people are looking for that same

opportunity? To simply be heard without judgement. Or maybe even....to hear their story and someone practice listening without judging. I bet the number is overwhelming.

That said, moving forward, that will be my approach toward building rapport and establishing friendship. So much of building rapport and establishing friendship is simply showing up and showing up consistently. And when I show up, leaving my snobbish hammer of guilt and conviction at my house and opening my heart to the rainbow-ish beauty that is the human spirit. And during this process, if I discover a jewel of a person, it'll be my gain. If I only get a bootyquake, at very least, I'll get a laugh.

List some areas in which you hope to become more understanding and open.

_____

_____

_____

_____

_____

_____

_____

_____

_____

_____

_____

_____

_____

LIST 19: ERRANDS

(December 16, 2015)

Five words/phrases that annoy me (probably more than they should) because of their subjective meaning(s)....

1. **"Errands". Either you have too many to list or you just don't want to tell me.**
2. "I don't know". Either you don't actually know or you know and just don't want to tell me.
3. "Kinda". Either you really don't know or you know and just don't want to tell me.
4. "Maybe". Either there are actually too many things to take into consideration or you have a real answer....and you just don't wanna tell me.
5. "Your guess is as good as mine." The only way to tell if this is actually true, is for you to actually guess, I guess....then to actually compare.

Bonus: "Actually". Whatever you say after this...is probably not actual, but maybe more general.

Jarred Pettijohn – "Here's one that annoys me the most. 'I could care less.' – This means that you care. If you didn't care, you 'couldn't care less' which is the correct way to say what you are intended to say."

Jeannie McMahan – "Ha. When I was a little girl I loved using the word 'actually'. I read once that people who say 'actually' may be lying. Actually, I don't care, because I like the word…"

Danni Dizzy – "You are ridiculous bro!!"

MaryBeth Omido – "Mmm, can I add to your comment about Actually--it can turn a compliment into an insult in an instant. 'You look good today.' vs 'You actually look good today.'"

Katy Janaye – Not that you asked, but words that annoy me are LITERALLY, when it's NOT literal compared to something figuratively. And anything EVER. Let's be honest, no one was around for the entire time of the whole universe so no one knows if it was the best, coolest, worst, etc., EVER."

Jennifer Thomas – "I'm surprised irregardless is not on the list because it is at the top of mine."

Andrew Hamm – "Bruh. Truth. And I feel convicted."

Pam Dehorney – "'Honestly' is the word for me. It implies that everything that was said previously to using the word 'honestly' was dishonest."

Cara McKenzie Fain Hardee – "I just laughed out loud."

THE STORY

"I have an errand to run." I have a friend that says this quite a bit. Part of it is because since she's not naturally a detail sharer, she automatically assumes everyone else isn't and probably shouldn't be one either. The other part is because she's secretive. This is not to be confused with being private. Private implies that I have personal business I don't want to share or should even feel obligated to share. Secretive means I am doing something I don't want people to know because of how I believe they will react.

One day, myself and a group of friends, which included her, are all sitting around having a good time. All of a sudden, she looks at her phone, begins to gather her things, then says, "Hey guys, I'll catch you later. I have a few errands to run." We all begin to look around at each with a mixture of amazement and disappointment because we thought we were all spending the day together. Where did this mystical errand come from?

Is it important enough to leave? Does it have to be done right now? Can we all go along on the errand so the fun can keep going? We poked fun, asked questions and asker her to stay, but she held to her errands and eventually left.

Exits like this, for her, was not an anomaly. These were regular exits.

THE OBSERVATION

When people are left to their own imaginations, without explanation, they can become pretty creative. You have those in the group who will allow their own personal experience to determine and dictate what's taking place within the secrecy of another's life. "I hope she's not going to [insert the worst possible dramatic decision she could make]." Then, you have those that don't think anything of it. If she says she has something to do, she simply has something to do. From those two groups, you have those who refuse to be offended because of the vagueness. This leaves the other part of the group that is highly offended because she won't share with the group what the errands are.

- "She doesn't trust us enough to share?"
- "It doesn't matter where I'm going, who I'm going with or what I'm about to do, I would tell my friends."
- "If she's not sharing with us, does that mean we aren't as close as we thought we were?"
- 'I'm going to say something the next time she does that."

Whoa! That's a pretty intense line of reasoning and questioning. Maybe that's why she doesn't say anything. Maybe she knows if she says something, people are going to jump all over her with unsolicited concern, advice and judgement. Maybe she's not going to do anything and she just needed a reason to leave. Maybe she's an introvert and it's time to recharge doing something she enjoys rather than the large social environment. No one knew and because they didn't, a few of them became consumed by their thoughts.

I'm sure everyone in the group would have appreciated a little more information about these infamous errands, but I wouldn't say we were owed information. I would also say that I don't think the sharing of that information was a prerequisite of being a part of the group.

Eventually, myself and another friend begin reaching out a little more consistently and in a smaller more intimate setting. We found out that "errands" sometimes meant dropping some things off at the post office, getting groceries, attending another social setting or catching her favorite show at home. However, most of the time "errands" meant there is someone in this room that consistently mistreats me and I've reached my limit. I tolerate it because I like hanging out with everyone else in the group, but once I reach my limit, it's time to leave. Instead of bringing attention to it, causing a tenseness within the group, possibly drawing lines of loyalty throughout the group or stirring up avoidable drama, it was easiest for her to leave.

We would have never known hadn't we cared for her as an individual, moved at her pace of sharing and been intentional with our approach.

THE LESSON

Her response to conflict caused me to look at my life. Do I run errands when things get thick? In church, when I disagree with the message or the leadership, do I tuck tail, zone out and disengage OR do I fight for understanding and commit to creating the change I believe others like me would benefit from? In the workplace, when the environment turns poison and I notice unethical behavior, do I return to my office and turn a blind-eye OR do I stand for what is right by addressing the people and behavior regardless of what it will cost me? In my community, when I see injustices and broken systems, do I only send my thoughts and prayers and hold close to those around me OR do I step outside the comfort of my own safety and pick up a cross that isn't mine?

I must admit. For quite some time, I have been an errand runner. Conflicts arise, I find something else I need to do.

Misinformation is passed around, I find something else to focus on. Emotional and physical abuse takes place, I say, "It's their business, not mine." Well, those days for me are coming to an end. Being present and living in the moment is where I choose to be. I'm sure real-life errands will often require my attention, but I won't use them as a means of avoidance.

Addressing conflict isn't easy. Standing in the face of disagreement is quite difficult. Opposing opposition isn't fun. I don't want to be disagreeable for disagreeing sake. I do it because someone HAS to do it. I get it. Voicing an unpopular, yet well thought out stance will get me some flack. BUT it will let people know where I stand and why I stand there. I don't have to run from social bullies. I don't have to fear the ignorantly loud. It's okay to point out the flaws and errors of the guy on the microphone. Accountability CAN be a standard for all people. Coach isn't always right. The teacher isn't always the smartest person in the room. Gossip isn't a social norm that I have to accept or participate in.

And when situations like these arise, I won't find an errand to run. I'm staying.

List some areas you plan to confront and from which you will no longer run.

_____

_____

_____

_____

_____

_____

_____

_____

_____

_____

_____

_____

LIST 20: HOLDING HANDS WITH A STRANGER

(December 9, 2015)

Strange things I've done in the past week with strangers....

1. Hugged a McDonald's worker for delivering awesome service.
2. **Held hands with a stranger at church.**
3. Shared a dessert with one of my wife's co-workers.
4. Confetti'd my wife's boss with wrapping paper at their Christmas party.
5. Touched pinkies with another man.
6. Scratched another man's beard.
7. Got honked at, cussed out and flipped off for texting and driving.
8. Became FB friends with a guy I met in a coffee shop. He's awesome!
9. Picked fuzz out of a stranger's hair.
10. Straightened a stranger's collar.

Billie Smith – "I am LOL at #9. I'm a touchy feely, even with strangers, so I'm guilty of picking lint off someone's shoulder. This whole list made me laugh!"

Andria Campbell – "Beautiful!"

Leah Shannon – "Stranger danger!"

Alan K. Swan – "busted."

Godlove Ngo – "Just another day in the life of Derrick."

Tequia Sier – "#7 please stay safe…and ALIVE. I need you!!! #3/4 – People always fall in love w/you no matter how outrageous you get. Stop encouraging him people! ;)"

Kimberly Pruitt-Zachery – "You Rock!!!"

Jerry MrWill Williams – "You are so random…Lmao"

Jason Zielke – "I stopped a bearded hipster and told him his fly was down."

Gina Michelle Henson Marshall – "You take 'Love thy neighbor' to a whole 'nother' level!!! Good job!"

THE STORY

My family and I have been at our current church a little over a year. We visited this church because we had a few trusted friends who attended there. We came, liked what we saw, enjoyed what we experienced and decided to make the leap to join their congregation. We had great plans to get involved and contribute our gifts to the corporate initiative of the church, but wanted to observe a bit more before committing fully.

Usually, during this time of observation and discovery, you will meet people who have been at the church for a bit longer than you have. As you are feeling them out, trying to get information about the church, they are feeling you out trying to figure out your gifts and how to get you plugged in. In a sense, your gift and/or interest will put you in a place which allows you to serve instinctively and intuitively, as it should be. My wife and I wanted to serve the community through outreach, but at the time, it was under-developed. This landed us into our secondary interest, which was still okay, just not ideal. For her, it was working with the children. For me, it was singing.

Practice was on Thursdays. This is when you get the new music, learn your parts, given direction for Sunday's delivery and hang out with the people you'll be serving alongside. That was my favorite part, serving alongside the people. I've never considered myself a strong vocalist. And because of that, I don't think I've ever really enjoyed singing like those who identify themselves as singers. For me, I can hold a note and people need people who can hold notes. That has always been the extent of my participation. However, I do love the atmosphere that music creates and with that environment comes some pretty cool people. I like people.

During this particular Thursday practice, toward the end, the director instructed everyone in the group to partner up with one other person. After we found someone to partner with, we spent some time hearing their story and praying for their needs. Of course, I was eager to partner with people I had already met. It's generally easier that way. As I locked eyes with a choir friend, I began to walk that way, but someone behind me grabbed my hand and stopped me dead in my tracks. I turned to find this older gentleman with his glasses hanging firmly to the tip of his nose and the warmest smile planted softly on his face. For the next 10 minutes, while holding hands, we learned how our lives overlapped and we learned of the needs existing between the two of us. I couldn't tell you what we prayed about that day. I can tell you that was probably the best and most fulfilling 10 minutes I've ever had at that church to date. He and I still speak frequently. And whenever we see each other, we shake hands.

THE OBSERVATION

I didn't even consider this guy as an option. We had been sitting in the same section all night, singing the same part. We sat by each other and only exchanged pleasantries. I would hand him a sheet of music as it was passed down the row. He was doing the same for me when the sheet music came from the other end. We didn't ask each other about singing parts or notes. We didn't talk about the weather. I didn't ask him about his day nor did he about mind. In fact, this day was the first time I had even seen him up close. I always saw him from a distance. Yet, here we are. Two strangers holding hands. Finding commonalities. Sharing semi-transparent needs with each other. And it worked out perfectly. I'm sure if all of my other options would have been taken and we were the last two to pair up, we would have done just fine. But the way we paired has a lot to do with the moment. And it worked perfectly.

It would have been hard to imagine this night playing out the way it did. Yet, I wouldn't have had it any other way. If someone would have told me the day before:

"You see that man? Tomorrow, after choir practice, you two are going to hold hands, exchange stories, swap needs, pray for each other and it's going to be the moment that catapults you into serving well at this church. That moment is going to stand head and shoulders above any other experience you're ever going to have with this congregation."

…I would have received it with great skepticism, for multiple reasons. I have no relationship with this man. We had not exchanged two words before that day. He is definitely unassuming. There is nothing about him that stands out. Does he even hold a position at this church? My external observation would have lead me to overlook this man in every area of life. In fact, my assumptions almost caused me to miss out on a wonderful experience.

THE LESSON

I can look back over my life and see multiple people and opportunities I've overlooked because of my inability to look past their cover. How often have I gravitated toward the big, fun, lively, attractive group instead of the smaller, quiet and intimate setting? And vice-versa? How many times have I waited to confirm the smaller lesser paying group because there is a larger higher paying group nibbling at the hook? How many times have I chosen to mentor the easier kid, tackle the sexier project, work with the smartest cohorts, check on my car every five seconds because of the neighborhood, hope to not sit next to "that person" on the plane, not attend "that church"….this list goes on, unfortunately.

Now, I can hear many of my readers thinking, "Sometimes, those quick external judgements are based on truths and can save you a bit of hassle or even your life." There is some truth to that. However, I believe those occurrences are few and far in between (with the exception of certain high-risk professions).

I'm talking day to day life. I believe we spend more time basing the crux of our interactions on external stimuli. This means we only get the surface of who people really are. We determine their character based on individual and isolated comments. We chalk up their personality to a single response. We take an isolated behavior and transfer it across every area of their life. Ironically, we'd be disappointed and feel cheated if people did the same thing to us. I know I would.

Even worse, we take the actions of a few and place it on the intentions of others. Because of the way this one pastor treated me, all pastors must be like him. Insert any culture, race, sexual preference, gender, economic status, private/public school student, athlete, artist...the list goes on. We have become content with lumping people together instead of getting to know them as individuals. And you don't have to tell me, grouping is easy and individuality is hard. It takes work to get to know a person for themselves; to differentiate them from the people that look, sound, talk, walk like them and come from the same place. BUT the reward of individuality is so much sweeter.

Initially, I didn't give this older gentleman a chance, but he gave me one. I don't know. Maybe he pressed pass the discomfort of his assumptions of my age, dress, race and the few character differences he observed during rehearsal to give me chance. Maybe he didn't want to partner with me as much as I didn't want to partner with him. But it happened. He reached out, stopped me from doing what I've always done and opened my eyes to a whole new experience....simply by holding this stranger's hand.

In most cases, I'm a hugger. In this case, I choose to be a hand holder. I am choosing to not only reach outside of my comfort zone of habits, but also outside of fear, doubt, rejection, assumption, prejudice, racism and preference. I choose to reach out and grab the hands of those with whom I want to do life. I want to expose myself to the lives of others and give them the opportunity to expose themselves to my life. Let's get to know each other. Let's exchange needs and concerns. Let's address them together....and we can even hold hands while we do it.

List some uncomfortable areas you are making into your new comfort zone.

_____

_____

_____

_____

_____

_____

_____

_____

_____

_____

_____

_____

LIST 21: WHAT'S IN YOUR HAND?!

(December 4, 2015)

Mentorship in disguise.
Domino Lessons:

---

1. All money ain't good money.
2. Decisions now effect you later.
3. **Make the best of what's in your hand.**
4. Know your opponents/teammates.
5. Never talk crap to your mentor. You won't win
   another game. Ever. Ever.

Jawan Johnson – "Wise lessons sir."

THE STORY

I mentor a group of boys at one of the high schools/career techs in Oklahoma City. What makes this group of students different and unique is many of them have been removed from their home schools. I say removed, but that can imply several different things. They could be more free form learners and unable or unwilling to adapt to the structure of the traditional high school setting. They could also be at this location because they are interested in acquiring training for a trade over the traditional route to employment through the educational system. They could also be here as a result of their disruptive behavior and poor decision making. In fact, this could be their final stop before being assigned to an alternative school or a GED program. It's definitely a unique crew. So, when given the opportunity to head up this program, I leaped at it.

One of the cool, and equally difficult, things about

mentoring is finding new, current and relevant ways to connect. You can't get preachy or they'll tune you out. You can't get too corny or they'll tune you out. You can't take a close-minded and short-sided approach or they'll tune you out. In fact, you're lucky if they only tune you out. That means they stayed, but aren't listening. I've been in mentor groups where mentees have stood up and walked out based on their lack of interest. I haven't had that yet. I'm been fortunate enough to stay ahead of their boredom curve.

Often times, I'll use games as an avenue for discussion. We'll spend most of our time together playing the game and end the day with some life lessons as it pertains to some of the concepts within the game. This particular day, we were playing dominoes. The concept I wanted them to learn was "Make the best of what's in your hand."

THE OBSERVATION

Whenever I play games with my boys, I often find them either taking all of the credit for their success or blaming others for their lack of success. This either/or mentality deduces: if I succeed, it was because I did well. If I don't succeed, it was because someone else didn't do well. I'll put it another way. The only reason I can't succeed is because of someone else. I see them carry this mentality into their personal, financial, social, familial, communal, educational and romantic areas of their lives as well.

Anytime I hear this type of conversation happening or see this type of thinking beginning to take root, I address it. This is not something I want to manifest in multiple areas of their lives. True, there are some things that happen to them that are outside of their control. Regardless of that occurrence, I want them to know that they have the power and ability to make the best out of every situation.

It doesn't matter what school they attend, the sport they play, the people in their classroom, the amount of money their parents make, the side of town they live on, whoever is in whichever political office, the clothes they wear....they must have the understanding they can influence and control the outcome of their situation. Just because their situation is that way now, doesn't mean it has to stay that way tomorrow. They can make the best out of what's in their hand today. How do I know they can? It has been done before. It's still happening as we speak. People all over the world are overcoming tremendous odds to accomplish their goals. People just like them are utilizing everything at their disposal to become the best they can be. They can do it too.

THE LESSON

Hollywood has made movies about it. Musicians have written songs about it. There are professional across a myriad of profession sharing their stories about it. People have and will continue to make the best out of whatever is in their hand. The earlier my mentees can grasp that concept, the better off they will be. Why will they be better? They will see every setback as an opportunity to launch forward. They will see every opposition as an opportunity to show strength. They will see every obstacle as moveable, every mountain as climbable, every wall as destructible and every closed door as openable.

Sure, you can waste your time dreaming you had a different hand or you can seize the moment and dominate the day. Be creative. Be strategic. Bluff if you have to. But what you can't do is freeze, refuse to play this game of life or blame others for your lack of success. That kind of thinking is a slippery slope that leads to a pit of helplessness, pity, regret and self-hate. That slope is hard to climb. That pit is difficult to escape

Fifteen. Your turn.

List some of your skills, gifts and talents for which you are grateful.

_____

_____

_____

_____

_____

_____

_____

_____

_____

_____

_____

_____

_____

_____

LIST 22: HARD TO TAKE

(December 2, 2015)

Random thoughts/moments....

1. I'm always curious to see who's that one mutual friend. Smh...
2. I was almost hit by a lady who was putting on make-up, eating breakfast, smoking and talking on the phone while driving.
3. I love it when I meet a social media "friend" in person! Like...I LOVE IT!
4. I had a kid say to me, "You that good kinda different tho." Me: "Thanks?!"
5. I feel asleep in a coffee shop today.
6. I walked into gym class and grabbed a ball. One of the high school kids said, "What you gon' do with that ball, old man?" I proceeding to hoop them kats in slacks and Stacy Adams.
7. My wife (is fine) finished my home office over Thanksgiving break. #realmvp
8. I got to love on Jerel and Sunshine today (hugs and convo). Two of the most positive and consistent people (professors/friends/colleagues) I know. Super glad they're in my life.
9. **My Dream Coach, Gregory Heady Coleman, gave me some advice/instruction yesterday. It was hard to take. I'm so glad he's straight up with me.**
10. Who wants to bring their chainsaw over to my house and help me get rid of these big branches in my yard?!?!

Kimberly Pruitt-Zachery – "#1 I can't help with cutting the tree but I can bring over one of the patty pies and some coffee."

Sunshine Ponder Cowan – "We loved seeing you – but the visit was too short."

Robin Summers Gonzalez – "#4 though! Best way to be, my friend!"

Briana Steelman – "My favorite post always in my news feed! Don't stop!"

Alicia Douglas Rambo – "No chainsaw here, but I do have two arms and two legs that are pretty good at hauling and stacking the branches after they've been cut..."

Marcellus Coleman – "#2 – is it wrong if I'm mad and impressed by her at the same time??"

THE STORY

Gregory Coleman is on my super hero list. He is one of the few and consistent people in my life who pushes me like his success depends on it. Whether it's sending an early morning scripture or sending flat out unsolicited and preventative correction, he is consistent, straight forward, loving and directional with his friendship. I hope I never take this for granted. And I wouldn't have it any other way. Well, maybe I would have he and his beautiful family live closer to mine, but that's about it. I wouldn't change anything else.

This particular day, I was complaining about someone to Gregory and he stopped me right in the middle of my statement and said, "Maybe it's just you." I could and couldn't believe what he just said. "Maybe it was just me?" However, I could understand if anyone would say something like that, it would be him. But the fact he said it caught me off guard. I'm not used to people calling me out like that. I secretly wish it would happen more often because now I'm beginning to think how many people in my life pander or pacify me. On the other hand, I'm not sure if my pride, ego, feelings could handle feedback like that often. BUT I know I need it. SO, if I had to choose to receive the correction or not, I choose to have people call me out when I'm missing the point, am being stubborn and bratty or just being plain ol' stupid.

I'm not sure whether the statement was strategically placed or not, but Gregory conveniently had to step away and we weren't able to finish the conversation until another time. However, during that break in our conversation, his statement forced me to pause and take a look at myself. What was I saying? How could I be so accusatory? Why did I choose to use those words to describe the moment and the people associated with it? Why were my feelings so hurt about it? Why was I so emotionally ramped up and involved? Why did I lack the understanding, grace, mercy and empathy with which I crave for people to handle me? I was being harsh, coarse and sharp in tone and character. Gregory called me on it.

When Gregory attempted to finish the conversation, I stopped him and told him I had already resolved it. His brave and direct reaction to my action saved the day. Had he not corrected me and caused me to pause; had he pumped me up by being a "yes friend" in that moment, I would have left that conversation, contacted the people with whom I had an issue and completely embarrassed myself. The correction was medicine: hard to take but necessary for my health.

THE OBSERVATION

I've found, it's more often how you say something rather than what you say. Gregory could have struck out with his feedback several different ways. If he had been softer with his reply, I would have talked right through it. If he had tip-toed around it and been vague in his feedback, I wouldn't have understood the severity of it and completely missed the point he was trying to make. Had he been calloused and flippant in his response, I would have been offended and still missed the heart of his statement. Instead, he took advantage of his access into my life, the history and rapport we've developed over time and his understanding of how I am built so he could concoct the perfect cocktail of correction and direction.

Another thing he was able to do was remove his friend, big brother and advocate hat and be what I needed in the moment, which was a coach. I don't know that I do that well or do it too often...be what people need in the moment. Honestly, I don't know how many people in my life are able to do that as well for me as Gregory has done over the years. I have a few close friends who do it well in social situations; they may dabble with input in other areas. My wife does it well as it pertains to our relationship and family, and also dabbles. But Gregory wears multiple hats in our relationship and probably has the most access, equal in all areas of my life. None more than the other, but equally. He uses his access well.

THE LESSON

I don't know that one person should have access to every area of your life. I do know we should surround ourselves with people who collectively have access to every area of our lives. I'll say it in a different way. If you have five friends, between all five of those friends, you should be held accountable in every area of your life. Financial. Spiritual. Social. Political. Romantic. Intellectual. There should be no area of your life to which you should be able to retreat and remain unreachable.

Let's be clear. This is a lesson on accountability, not independence or individuality. Should you be able to do whatever you want without the say so of others? Of course. Should you be able to make decisions and hold yourself accountable to those decisions? Heck yeah! Date whoever you want? Live where you want? Work where you want. Buy whatever you want? Travel the world by yourself? Explore religion and spirituality? Yes to all of those. However, I don't believe any single person holds the entire perspective to every situation. Sometimes...well, most times, we need the external perspective of a few. A few folks who are looking at the situation from the outside.

When getting the design finalized for this book, Kristen said, "I know you are going to send this to several people for feedback. Just remember a couple of things. You are never going to please everyone and at the end of the day, YOU have to be pleased with the product." She never said to NOT poll my circle or to NOT get external feedback because that would have been foolish. If I would have chosen my first book cover on my own, I would have chosen a cover I would have hated a month after production. Seriously! I was looking at that option the other day and thought, man…I'm glad I polled my circle. Ha!

The same goes for you. With whom are you discussing ideas? Have you introduced that person you're dating to your friends and family? What about that new job you're considering? Have you ran that by anyone? What about that city you were thinking about visiting, that outfit you're considering purchasing or that neighborhood you're about to move into? Are you able to make all of those decisions on your own? Of course! Are you willing to live with the results of those decisions? I'm sure you are. Are there other ways to make the best and most informed decisions besides making them yourself? I would argue yes.

Be an adult. Of course. Do you. But include others along for the ride. They'll come in handy. Promise.

List some feedback that was hard to take, but you needed to hear.

_____

_____

_____

_____

_____

_____

_____

_____

_____

_____

_____

_____

_____

_____

_____

LIST 23: LOSING 12-0

(November 28, 2015)

A few lessons I learned from my son's soccer team today....

1. **Losing 12-0 teaches you more about your kid than him/her winning 12-0.**
2. Parents are way more into the game than their children.
3. Sportsmanship is subjective.
4. The coach-athlete relationship is more important than I thought.
5. Learning to do something "good" will only get you so far.
6. Every moment is a teachable moment.
7. High fives and chest bumps can be fun or annoying....depending on which side of the score board you are on.
8. Playing is the greatest compliment to/supplimental for adulting. Kids soon will learn.
9. Parents should be, at the least, knowledgeable of whatever their kids are involved in. Be able to talk about it with confidence.
10. Someone should write a book entitled, "101 Things I Learned from Being a Sports Parent".

Brad Davis – "You have 10 down so add 91 more and your book is complete."

Mark Johnson – "A book? You've only got 91 more to go...."

Hannah Lee De Ojeda – "I've got one for your book! Winning as a team is more fun than winning by yourself. Reb got third in both her swimming relay and the individual backstroke event. She was so much more excited about placing in the relay even though the relay was 3rd out of 5 teams and backstroke was 3rd out of 15 swimmers. Kids don't evaluate it like that though. It's just fun to win with your friends. :)"

Gregory Coleman – "[…] I'm always more interested in my son learning to coach the game than playing. More opportunities when his playing days are over. #DreamCoach #LifeCoach #SportsCoach #BusinessCoach

Leon Fowler – "Oh man I could help you write that book!! Worst thing to do is not show up for games. OR missing most of the games and promising them you will be there at the next one and just not show up."

Sonia Cavazoz – "Luv this!!!! Having 2 boys in sports can be very nerve wrecking. I literally read a book on Football & Basketball so I could understand better & let me tell you… years later I have the most INTENSE convos w my sons! […] A coach/athlete is the GREATEST thing because they so LISTEN! Trust me! Great job, Derrick!"

Marcellus Coleman – "I've observed No. 7 from the perspective of the losing team. It's so discouraging for children to see the winning team, get affirmed by their parents; while they themselves see the following responses: 1 – wow the coach sucked 2 – they should have played my kid 3 – you didn't do good enough 4 – better luck next time."

Rachael Fugate – "13 years and counting being a sports parent. […] You learn a lot about yourself! The good and bad. The one thing I know I did right was always be there."

Sara Carreno – "Sports were my life as a kid. As a parent I'm already burnt out. The drama and race to the top is too much!"

THE STORY

My son has bounced from interest to interest over the years. Drums. Gymnastics. Basketball. We finally landed on soccer. He was good. Naturally good. He loved to run. He liked being on a larger team. I think it relieved some of the pressure on him as an individual player. We started out playing in a church league. Then some of the other parents noticed him. Then we moved to an indoor league. We were noticed by a few of the other parents there as well. Then we joined an outdoor academy team and then another team, which landed us here with a competitive club in South OKC. With each change, the sport became more competitive and the players were more skilled.

We were a pretty good team playing under a new coach. Usually, what happens when you are good at one level, the team opts to play up an age group. This usually comes with playing larger more skilled opponents. In this particular tournament, our team was significantly humbled to the tune of 12-0. That means we lost by twelve goals and we didn't score one. The athletes on the other team had been playing longer. They were smarter. They were faster. They were taller and longer. They were stronger. Overall, they were just a better team. Simple as that. Lesson learned. The next tournament, we played back down against other kids our age. Those games were a lot more fun to watch. And when I say fun, I mean the games were more even regarding skill level.

THE OBSERVATION

While losing handedly, my focus turned from the score to the response of the players on our team. Some players had completely given up. They stopped hustling after the ball. Their passes were lazy. They stopped defending and would jog instead of run. Some other players started to play dirty and foul the other team. I guess they took it personal the other team continued to score instead of ease up a bit. The remaining players played their heart out until the last whistle. They ran their hardest, chased and defended; took shots when open and stayed dialed into the game as if they still had a chance. If I had to put my money where my mouth was, in 10 years, I would hire those few kids that fought until the end and build a company on their fortitude and resilience.

Now, I know it's soccer, but ball is life. You can identify the cheaters. The hard workers. The ones determined to slide by on natural talent and a good personality. You can see the team players. The ones whose parents are trying to live through them and are constantly faced with extreme expectations. You can tell the ones who believe they don't have anything else in life. You can tell the ones who are light years ahead of their teammates in the way they see and process the game. You know the ones who practice and handle their sport away from the field/court. I know we are talking about soccer, but I honestly believe ball is life.

THE LESSON

I honestly believe the things we learn as children carry over into our adulthood. Some of them are subtle, while others are blatant. This is why, as parents, we may appear to nag and be hard on the simplest of things, but it's because we want to nip that crap in the bud as soon as we see it. Pick up your clothes. Wash your hands. Brush your teeth. Did you do your homework? Be polite. Do your chores. Don't watch that on television. No social media just yet. I don't care what they do at Becky's house! Don't spend all of your birthday money at once. Firm hand shake. Make eye contact. Hold the door for your mother.

It's the same on the field during competition. I remember a soccer game in which a few of my son's teammates got mad at him. It was toward the end of the game. We were winning. My son and an opposing player were going for a ball and it went out of bounds. The referee said it went off the opposing kid's foot and awarded our team the ball. My son ran up to the official and said it should be their ball. The referee shook my son's hand and awarded the other team the ball. The players on the same side of the field as my son were vocally and physically upset with the decision made by my son and the referee. The game went on. We won. The players lined up to shake hands and then went back to their opposing benches.... with the exception of the head coach of the other team. He followed my son over to me. He shook my hand and said, "Classy kid. Whatever you're doing at home, keep doing it."

Winning doesn't develop character, it simply reveals it. What the majority of our team showed when they were down by 12 goals wasn't a result of the moment, it was a result of what was practiced at home. These kids didn't act out of character, they did exactly what was instilled in them to do. Their behavior wasn't an outlier. It was at the heart of who they were. And if it isn't checked as a young person, these are going to be adults who behave the same way under pressure.

Come on, you know that person at your job. You know that person who lives down the street from you. The person in the Wal-Mart line. You know that teacher or family member.... who pouts when things don't go their way. The person who takes their metaphorical ball and goes home. You don't have to think too hard to identify several people in your immediate and daily surroundings who make you think, "Man, I wonder what they were like when they were a kid?! Geez!" I'm right there with you. And while we're at it, we need to make sure we aren't those people as well. Truth.

It's not the good times that make up the core of who you are. It's the bad times. It's the low times. It's those times when you have to swallow your pride, take a loss, do great things with a little or something with nothing. Those are the times when you get to show yourself, the people around you and the world awatching, that your character can sustain you through the darkest and most difficult times. As for the future and the people who will await us there and are supposed to be the back bone of our society, we don't even have to look far into the future to see who and what awaits us there. We can go to a youth soccer game and watch the team losing 12-0.

List some things you heard as a child that has helped you in your life today.

_____

_____

_____

_____

_____

_____

_____

_____

_____

_____

_____

_____

_____

_____

LIST 24: KIDS SLEEP

(November 23, 2015)

I love it when.....

1. People hug me!
2. I hear my kids laugh.
3. **I hear my kids sleep.**
4. My wife and I hold hands while I drive.
5. I positively impact someone.
6. I see couples kiss.
7. I come home and smell food.
8. Friends shoot me random love texts.
9. I cry-laugh.
10. I see justice.

Thai Wong – "I love your bear hug, brother, I know it sounds awkward, but you make all the troubles melt away when you give me that smile with your arms wide open. Thank you for making possible change in all our lives."

Alex Mott – "That's a good list bro."

Briana Steelman – "I'm so glad we're friends!"

Phillis Tyson – "I love your positive postings they make me smile"

Kristi Clingenpeel Maxwell – "You are the best hugger!!!!!"

THE STORY

The house we currently live in is a fairly nice-sized house for our standards. 2200 square feet. Two-car garage with an extended driveway. Three beds. Two and a half baths. Living room. Den. Formal dining. Kitchen. Breakfast nook. Wash room. Loft. Back patio with a hot tub. Sprinkler system. When we moved into this house, minus missing an extra bedroom, it was everything we wanted. It was in a great neighborhood. Solid school system. Down the street from the our church, shopping, entertainment....everything we wanted. Couldn't have asked for anything more...with the exception of an extra bedroom. Ha!

The layout of the house put all of the bedrooms on the same hallway. Coming from the main area of the house and into the hallway, you would pass my son's room, my daughter's and walk straight into the master suite. In addition to all of the rooms being back to back to back, the hallway floor was tile and the walls were pretty thin. This means sounds traveled pretty easily from the master suite past the bedrooms and to the end of the hallway...unobstructed...efficiently. So much so, when everyone was settled in bed and the entire house was quieted, I could lay in my bed and hear my children breathing while they slept.

This became one of my most favorite things to do when winding down for the night. I could listen to them sleep forever.

THE OBSERVATION

When I was younger, my mother would come into the room to make sure I was breathing. She would tell me stories about waking up late at night multiple times just to make sure I was still breathing. I didn't know this was absolutely normal for parents to do. In fact, many parents won't even go to sleep until they know their children are down for the count and resting well. For the overly cautious, they put a baby monitor in the crib or bed of their child and the receiver wherever they were moving throughout the house. I had a friend that, for a while, could only go to sleep to the sound of her babies breathing. I was no different.

I don't know what it is about hearing your child resting soundly that brings about a calm unlike any other. Maybe it's the idea of them being safe and sound with full bellies having sweet dreams. Maybe it's the reassurance of having done something well for another day. Maybe it's the continual reminder that in a world full of chaos and noise, the sound of a sleeping baby becomes a fortress of comfort, a refuge of hope and reminder of all of things good in the world. Whatever it is, I want a double dose of it.

Sometimes, hearing them from a distance just wouldn't be enough. My wife would awake in the middle of the night to find me sleeping on their bedroom floor. I remember many times when I wasn't even sleepy, but the comfort, rhythmic breathing and peacefulness while holding my sleeping beauties would put me sound asleep right along with them. The gravitational lull of a sleeping baby...or deeply breathing children is unlike any other. I dare someone to resist its lure.

THE LESSON

I think I've narrowed it down. At the end of the day, when my children are asleep in the comfort and safety of their beds, I feel accomplished as a parent...as a provider and protector. I also feel the same way with my wife. When she's sound asleep and there is no strife between us, I feel more accomplished as a husband. The same with any scenario to which I'm attached which lends itself to operating smoothly and within a rhythm. There is something comforting about it. There is something reassuring about it. It breathes an air of confidence and accomplishment. Whenever I walk into a situation and everything is running smoothly, it reminds me of watching my babies sleep...listening to them breathe.

You know, there are very few things I wouldn't do to make sure my kids get that opportunity every single night. I'd wash a thousand loads of laundry. I'd clean a million dishes. I'd cut acres of grass and step on a million legos. I'd work another job and bust my tail getting to athletic events and theater shows.

Because at the end of their day, I need them worrying about one thing only, resting so they can be awesome tomorrow.

I wonder what people would do for a similar peace? How can something as simple as sleeping like a baby be coveted across the world. And it's not the actual sleep, but the security which allows them to sleep as such. Children aren't supposed to worry about bills and jobs and violence and wars and politics. Their thoughts shouldn't be consumed with body image, bullying, the cost of living and luxury tax. We take that responsibility for them. Well, if we carry all of the weight, who eventually carries it for us? What allows us the opportunity to sleep like babies? When do our friends and family get to peek inside our minds and see us resting comfortably, peacefully, safely in our homes and beds?

Rest isn't only for the babies. We must fight for peace as well. And until we get it, may everyone be blessed with the opportunities to rest vicariously through hope. As for me, I'm going to walk down the hall and peek into the rooms of two of the most precious gifts of hope…and listen to them sleep.

List some things that help ground you and bring peace into your life.

_____

_____

_____

_____

_____

_____

_____

_____

_____

_____

_____

_____

_____

LIST 25: YOU'RE THE GUY

(November 18, 2015)

Just a few random moments....

1. I saw two older black ladies laughing super hard in their car....driving 25 mph down NW Expressway. Not a care in the world..... I was jealous... and mad. (I was late to work!)
2. My son saw me with my shirt off and said, "That's a deeeeeeeeep belly button!" Haha! Jerk.
3. I stepped on a scale for the first time in three years. Got sad. Then went to the fridge and grabbed a Snickers Ice Cream bar.
4. I met a 6th grader that will be 14 in December. Eh hem... this means he'll be 20 when he graduates high school.
5. My daughter wore a certain pair of "pants" to school. When we got home, I asked her about them. She said, "Mom said they were fine. And remember, you can't talk about girl stuff." And so it begins.... grrrrrr!!!!
6. I cried while talking to a teacher about our students. It was refreshing and sad at the same time. I love her passion and commitment. I empathize with her frustration. (Parents, get involved!)
7. **I love it when kids recognize me out in public. Even more so when their parents say, "So you're the guy they are always rambling about." Impact, not pride.**

8. I had a friend tell their boss about me and my company. I'm now scheduled to work their leadership retreat this month. See how easy that was?!?! *hint*
9. I walked into a pizza place. Saw a kid I've been working with for the last two years. He bought my family a pizza. Respect! (Impact....not pride)
10. I've often struggled with having to choose between making money and truly serving people. My hope is that one will make way for the other....and eventually, I won't have to choose.

Bonus: My wife is fine! All day! Every day! Supa fine!

Drea AP – "You are one of THE most awesome souls I have ever had the fortune of meeting!! Thank you for these types of posts!"

Victor Viney – "Yes…"

Billie Smith – "I LOVE these posts because I relate to everyone last one of them! Mom to a teenager, girl even, AND working with the similar student situations on the daily. I cried just last week when an 8th grade girl talked about her mom staying in bed for days, depressed and drinking. How do you shake something like that off? You don't. You apply it when struggling with #10. Have a fabulous day!"

Mel Gaines Smith – "These posts of yours always make my day!!!!"

Jaime Taylor – "#4: gotta love the 3rd grade retention law! You're so funny--I look forward to these posts. And your wife IS precious!!"

Shayne Peffer – "You're my favorite!! I miss you!!"

Nicki French – "I would buy your book :-)"

Marcellus Coleman – "I love this. Thank you for posting this. Makes my day."

Lashonda Malrey-Horne – "As usual another great post. And your daughter is right, you can't talk about girl stuff. […] You can't say anything. Her momma will take care of it!"

Mitzi Dawn Smith – "Keep em coming! Love these updates."

Heather McFarland – "I ALWAYS enjoy reading these! Your perspective and soul is one of a kind!"

Cara McKenzie Fain Hardee – "SNICK. ERS. ICE. CREAM. SNICK. ERS. ICE, CREAM. SNICKERS ICE CREAM."

Laura Ragon – "I hope you are saving these to publish for a book one day soon."

Sarah Odusi – "Start a book of your random moments."

Michelle Cullen – "Always choose serving people/ That's a no brainer. Trust me there will come a day and you reflect back and will be glad you choose people over chasing money."

Chris Snoddy – "Love it!"

Mark Johnson – "Keep em' coming!"

THE STORY

Doing community work is hard. I don't care what people say or how gloriously they try to frame it, it's hard. It's dirty. It's gritty. Community workers must work with longsuffering in their heart…with the end in mind. They are often underpaid while living their professional lives on the front lines of the community and handling with compassion everything that comes with that demographic. Working in the community, you must have a long-term commitment and attachment to the end goal which can be decades down the line. Community workers must have an impenetrable and undefeatable love for people and genuinely desire to see the best in everyone regardless of what they show you. It is not for the faint of heart. I must not be done for personal gain and manipulative motives. Without social servants, the pulse of the community turns weak and the heartbeat which once echoed throughout the walls of the city will eventually fade. That's how important community workers are.

As difficult as it may be, many times the clouds will part, the haze will fade and something great and awesome happens which makes you remember why you opted into this line of work in the first place. One of the most memorable moments for me was when I ran into the parent of one of the students I had been working with for a couple of years.

I was in the store with my kiddos buying some groceries. When, out of nowhere, this little human rams into me and hugs my leg. Of course, I pause because the little humans with me are much taller than my leg. Which means the little human on my leg belonged to someone else. I looked down and recognize the school uniform from one of the schools I work with, but haven't yet seen the face in order to place the person. As this little person finally leans back, I see her face and look up in enough time to see the child's mom walking toward us. Of course, I quickly reached out my hand to introduce myself and my children. Once she heard my name, she softened her look of concern. Apparently, her daughter comes home singing the songs we teach her at school and tells her about our words of the week. Her response, "So, you're the guy they are always rambling about." Guilty as charged.

THE OBSERVATION

This isn't the first time a student has come up to me in public. In fact, it happens quite often. The only different between those times and this time is the parent came over the talk to me. I'm sure it had a lot to do with the age of the child and maybe even more so, me being a male. Regardless of the reason, the mother came over, spoke, we connected and she was able to see, first-hand, someone who was positively investing healthy nuggets of information and relationship into her child.

This should happen all of the time. Not so much the investment. Yes, that should be a regular, in fact, a daily occurrence. But I'm talking about the teachers/mentors interacting with the parents....in a positive way. Seeing the two interact shouldn't surprise anyone, but it does. Now-a-days, the only time the parent steps foot into a school or interacts with a teacher is when something is wrong. Parent-teacher interactions should be highly encouraged. Better yet, they should be partners in education with the student/child being the primary benefactor of the relationship. Schools should be getting more and more creative on facilitating the interaction between the two. Education should be a family experience as well as an institutional experience.

THE LESSON

When forces combine for good; to surround the student with love, support, compassion, understanding and resources, there is no limit to what can be achieved. This isn't isolated to the educational arena only. Children should receive support in every other area of life as well. That's the only way they can become the well-rounded individuals we all want them to be. For some reason, we expect them to complete the puzzle without being given the pieces.

My parents, as good as they were, never had the birds and the bees talk with me. For that reason, I was forced to create a picture of romance and intimacy based on the pieces society, Hollywood, pop culture, society and the information my friends gave me. I can tell you now as an adult, that was not the best way for a young man to discover romance and intimacy. While I am using students, children and the educational system as a platform from which to jump, the same can be said for any area in which people are trying to advance and progress.

There are many areas of life in which I felt like I was trying to advance and progress...as if I was trying to build a picture without the proper pieces. What ended up happening? My picture was flawed and I was set back time and time again. When we give someone the correct pieces and a clear picture of what can be, we set them far ahead of where they would have been had we not helped them.

In the store, I met a parent who was just as excited about my contribution to the life of her daughter as I was to see a parent actively engaged in the growth and advancement of their child. From that moment on, whenever I saw that parent, we exchanged pleasantries with the understanding we were on the same team and her child was the primary focus. This concept is transferable and should be applied to every area of our lives and the lives of those around us. As some point, we should all be the guy.....

List some areas in which you are able to be an example for others.

_____

_____

_____

_____

_____

_____

_____

_____

_____

_____

_____

_____

_____

_____

LIST 26: LOVE

(November 14, 2015)

As I scroll down my timeline, my friends look like...

1. Christian, Atheist, Agnostic, Buddhist, Jewish, Afrikan Centered....
2. Black, White, Eqyptian, Latino, Japanese, Indian, Native American....
3. Men, women, transgender...
4. Single, Married, polyamorous...
5. Gay, lesbian, straight...
6. Wealthy, poor, middle class....
7. Trade-ready, degree'd, diploma'd...
8. Diseased, maimed, whole, skinny, fat....
9. High-fivers, huggers, fist bumpers....
10. Democrat, republican, independent, unaffiliated....
11. Potty mouths and encouragers...
12. Athletic, scientific, artistic...
13. Highly reserved and highly sexual....
14. Teenagers, middle-aged, baby boomers and toddlers....
15. Ex-girlfriends, former enemies, people I've met on planes or during jury duty....
16. Thieves, liars and adulterers; philanthropists, civil servants and priests.
17. Company men and entrepreneurs...
18. Hopeless romantics and scorned hearts...
19. Hopeful and hopeless....

.....and I love every bit of it...every bit of you. Regardless of the area with which you identify. There's love.

Judie Lavender – "Love it."

Tiffany Whisman – "I mean wow. Love."

Kimberly Pruitt-Zachery – "Gotta love it!!!"

Jennifer Bridges – "I love your posts!!!!"

Marya Byers – "I love you Derrick Sier and this is why! U are an amazing person!"

Heather Strong – "We love you back."

Robin Summers Gonzalez – "Exactly how I feel my friend. I don't judge people. I don't presume to do my Savior's job. Love you to pieces"

Mandy Duane – "Blessed to know you!!"

Brad Brown – "Sounds like a man with a platform! Love = truth. Truth = Gospel. Gospel = Love. Sometimes love doesn't = P.C."

THE STORY

Depending on who you ask, the world is in a different place. Its people and countries are either coming together like never before OR it's going to hell in a hand-basket. Depending on who you ask will also determine the reason why the world is in whichever place it's in. Some believe millennials will be the gatekeepers through which poverty and racism is eradicated. Others believe that same group of millennials will be the ones carrying the hand-basket. Some believe same-sex marriage will be the destruction of the solid foundation of society that is built through a balanced home. Others believe cheating spouses, absentee parenting and disobedient children will be the destruction of said structure. Open borders. Closed borders. Church and State. Go get a job. Work for yourself. People died so you can vote. Don't vote for this crap! Everyone has their opinion on what is happening to the world around us and many are willing to share who they believe is to blame.

And this is just from my newsfeed. I don't even know what yours looks like.

However, in the midst of all the negativity and (mis) information floating around the cyber universe, I choose to see beauty. It's not even a fight or a press to see it. It's everywhere! And I'm not being metaphorical or hypothetical with this statement. I see beauty in people and in the things they do.

I emcee'd the Equality Run hosted by Oklahoma City's Freedom Oklahoma. This event was created to honor a community friend that touched so many lives while living. On this day, for this event, people left the comfort of their own homes and paused their lives for a day to share thoughts about his wonderful life and to honor his family. Before the race began, one of the event hosts teared up talking about the meaning of the race. One of the local ministers shared some thoughts and prayed a prayer before the race and then ran the race herself. Throughout the race, you could hear people cheering and music playing. As people finished the race, you could see high fives and hugs being exchanged. Smiles and happy crying eyes filled the faces of everyone there. Before everything completely shut down, the event staff were notified of one person still on the course. As word made it around, participants began gathering back on the course to meet this person down the street so they could run with her across the finish line. Eventually, she made it and was able to honor her fallen friend by completing the race created in the memory of his name. THIS, my friends......is beauty.

I am so glad stories like this aren't an isolated occurrence on my timeline. They are frequent. They are the majority. I see diversity in love and living. I'll take that every day.

THE OBSERVATION

As a communicator, I keep working based on the satisfaction of my client. I work diligently beforehand to make sure I understand their expectations and I work just as hard making sure I can meet those expectations. One of the ways I determine if I understood and met those expectations is through evaluations. I can't speak for anyone else, but some of my most gut-wrenching moments come from reviewing evaluations.

As a people pleaser, I want to make sure everyone is happy. And no matter how much I pump myself up before reading those evaluations, I always get caught off guard. Which one catches me off guard? It's the one or two low ratings out of the bunch. Can anyone out there identify with me? I could receive 100 "we think Derrick is the best" evaluations and my focus will stick on the two that thought I sucked.

I worked for a company that did trainings throughout the community. They would send people to elementary schools, high schools, churches, even prisons…wherever there was a need for the training they provided, their employees would go. Before sending their employees out to these various locations, they would train them in the content…as would any legitimate company. The final part of the training would be for every participate to take a part of the content and present to the class as if they were the trainer. After each person presented, they would be evaluated by the trainers. After my turn to present, everyone in the room thought I was solid. However, there was one person who said I was too loud, too busy, all over the place and aggressive. He added, he felt his heart rate go up and wanted to lean back in his chair to get away from my voice. This impacted the way I presented for months.

This is the same with the squeaky wheels of our society.

Why do we allow the few to ruin our day…our week? Why do we allow them to change our perspective? Why do we allow the negative Nancy's to distract us from our lives of love and hope to focus on conspiracy and hate? Somehow… somewhere…based on the opinion of someone else and NOT a personal encounter, someone hates someone else. That's right. Read it again. People are hating people they've never met. They are hating cultures they've never visited. They are condemning lifestyles they refuse to explore. It's a shame and I refuse to be a part of it.

THE LESSON

As I scroll my newsfeed and scan my community, there is a lot of life being lived. It's being lived all different kinds of ways. And people are living it to the fullest...having a blast doing so. I'll admit, it's fun when my way of life lines up with another's way of life. We have more in common. There is less conflict. The interaction is smooth. However, my lifestyle doesn't often line up with the majority of people with whom I interact. Some may look at that and suggest I find new places to hang out and new people to hang out with. That couldn't be farther from the truth. Find a new church? A new job? A new city? A new state? I'd be running my entire life if I was looking for homogeny.

It's not about bending the knee of the world to your preference. It's about finding a common place where we can all bend a knee in unity toward one another. It's not about fighting to find the good. It's about fiercely protecting it from the doom and gloom believers who mistake progress and evolution as a direct threat against the sanctity of humanity. Beauty is all around us. It's not hard to see. What we can't do is allow our vision to be clouded by the few who degrade humanity's efforts toward the discovery of commonality. And please believe, in your efforts to communicate your heart's desire to unify your community and ultimately the world, someone will step back and misevaluate your effort as "poor" and "needs work". I encourage your to look toward the masses from which your support comes from and continue to be encouraged. Look around you. You'll find support and you'll see there's love.

List some of your areas of growth in which your support group is already strong.

_____

_____

_____

_____

_____

_____

_____

_____

_____

_____

_____

_____

_____

LIST 27: MENTORSHIP

(November 12, 2015)

A few...interesting moments from the last week or so.....

1. I was sitting in church and overheard a lady say, "..... and so I told my daughter, you better be glad I'm not black and whoop you in front of all your friends...."
2. I was sitting at a light. A car rolls up beside me. There's a little boy in the back seat. I wave. He pushes his glasses up his nose...and gives me the finger. We get to the next light....and he still has it up. Haha!!!
3. An older white lady held the door for me at a school. As I walked by, she said, "My...how the times have changed, huh?"
4. I recently had a conversation with an OKCPS administrator about having to choose between the quality of education and racial diversity amongst faculty, staff and the student population. His answer? If you want that, you're gonna have to leave OKCPS. #ouch #andheworksthere
5. I hugged a kid at work. She said, "I like your hugs. Wait...I think I just like putting my face on your belly. LOL!
6. **I had three new kids asked to join my mentorship class. Hecks yayuh!**
7. I was in my car and saw a couple trying to take a picture of themselves by a sign. I stopped. Got out. Asked them if I could take the picture for them. Got back in my car. I hope they remember that picture and story forever!

8. My son asked about getting his hair cut into a high-top. I said, "Cool! I had one of those when I was your age!" He said, "Nevermind." Buster. LOL!
9. #OMOS has picked up some new excited opportunities. I love being able to better the world around me.
10. I'm a hugger. I forget that the rest of the world doesn't hug. I met a teacher for the first time. I jumped in and hugged her. She said, "Do I know you?!" I said, "I don't think so." She said, "Ah well... nonetheless. Perfect timing. I've been having a crappy day and just thought....man I need a hug. And then you walked through the door. Thanks."

Katie Dow – "I always look forward to your posts!"

Sandy Goins-Pratcher – "Bonus! #mwif"

Cabrone Brewer – "Your high-top was on point back then though!"

Lindsey Jones – "Your weeks are super entertaining! #lifewithDerrickSier I think it should be a TV show"

Jessica Nilsen – "I too look forward to your posts! I'm a hugger too! Keep doing what you're doing!"

Jazman Nicole – "Huggers rule the world!"

Moheb Mark Atia – "Too bad that it's you that has to 'learn'. Keep smilin' that'll disarm the grumpy"

Julie Wade Crum – "#8 Kids keep us humble. Love your posts, Derrick Sier. I always read them to Andy so he can enjoy them too."

Rebecca Tyler – "Number 10 is sooooo me! The power of a great hug is magnificent!"

Jaime Taylor – "I love your hugs! And in my job, it's pretty much given that I will always need one!"

Noble Sandlin – "I'm a hugger too, Derrick Sier. It's the way I was raised!"

Sean Johnson – "#2 made me holler in the doctor's office….. Lol"

Mandy Duane – "These make my day. You should write a book."

Tamia Taylor – "I love you."

Shanon C. Norton – "Love these! It's awesome how observant u are!"

THE STORY

You've already read my perspective on how difficult I believe mentoring can be. So, when any of my current mentees recruit other people into the group, I consider it a compliment. Correction, I consider that more than a compliment, I consider it a victory. That's the purpose of mentoring, right? You are trying to not only impact a person, but somehow impact everyone attached to that person. In this case, I have been given the opportunity to impact their friends; a responsibility I don't take lightly and at the same time, an honor and a privilege.

On this day, we were preparing to play basketball. A few of my regulars came out and said, "Coach, can we invite a few friends to hang out with us? They've seen you around and heard about our class. They wanna hang too." Of course, I said yes! This is the equivalent of your kids bringing people over to taste your cooking. Heck yeah, they can come have a taste of what I'm cooking in this classroom! My only condition is they can't ball and leave. They have to commit to at least a month of my classes. They agreed, hooped, came for the month and stayed for the rest of the semester. WIN!

THE OBSERVATION

In *Small Stories, Big Team* I said, "People want to be a part of something people want to be a part of." I honestly believe that. In my mentorship class, it has always manifested as such. Sure, the faculty and staff identify and recruit the students to come, but it's my relationship with them and the hype around the class which keeps them coming back. And when I say hype, of course we have fun, but the real hype around the class is what I bring to the table. What do I bring? Energy. Acceptance. Judgement free environment. Commitment. Genuine love. Honesty. Feedback. Outside of the classroom interaction. Relatability. Relevance. Accountability. Not only do these things retain participants in a mentorship class, they also attract people in general.

All of those attributes are applicable across the board. Whether it is in relationship or business, people want to be a part of something people want to be a part of. Marriage. Friendship. Church. Housing community. Athletic team. School. A bank. Grocery store. A job. People are attracted to something bigger than themselves....something that will outlast their existence. All of those attributes do just that. How? Just like this.

One of my mentees called me the other day. He was a part of my very first group at this location. He said, "Coach, this year, I did something that I wouldn't have done last year. I set a goal and I accomplished it." I knew exactly which goals he was talking about because I helped him set those goals. At the beginning of the year, we determined he would pass his reading test, get his license, graduate high school, get a car and move into his own apartment. He did all of those. Without prompting him, he said, "I wouldn't have been able to do it without you hounding me, being honest with me, taking me places and keeping me encouraged. I love you for that, Coach."

THE LESSON

As a mentor, I'm doing more than recruiting and retaining kids into a classroom. I'm recruiting them to a lifestyle. I don't act a certain way to get something. I act that way all the time and acquire the things I pursue. I would even go a step further and say those things find me. The skills I teach and lifestyle

I model recruits people all by itself. When people see you are happy and they aren't happy, they'll ask you where you get your happy from. The same with money, education, influence, property, work, peace....you are the walking billboard for life. A few of my mentees caught the vision and now are role models for their friends and family.

In the same way we are drawn to things, people are drawn to us. The question is, to what are we drawn? I have a friend who loves pizza. He can smell it a mile away. When he sits down with a pizza, he eats the entire pizza. That same friend also loves success. Whenever he sets his mind on something, he doesn't stop until he achieves it. He knows what kind of food he wants. He knows what success looks like for him.

Who are you following? Why are you following them? Who's following you? Do you know why they are following you? I think these are all fair questions. When we are able to answer them, we will know where we are heading, why we are headed there and who's coming with us.

List your mentors and the area in which they mentor you.

_____

_____

_____

_____

_____

_____

_____

_____

_____

_____

_____

_____

_____

LIST 28: ENCOURAGEMENT ALWAYS WINS

(November 8, 2015)

A few lessons I learned from my son's four-game weekend of soccer....

1. There are always reasons to high five someone. We just have to find them.
2. Most of the time, he already knows what he did wrong before I remind him 1000 more times.
3. You can't want something more for someone...more than they want it for themselves.
4. **Encouragement always wins.**
5. Children will never really understand all that parents do for them...until the day they become parents.
6. In the same manner that hate is taught, so is cheating. Just a little bitter, yes
7. Every time I go to Edmond, I remember why I don't ever go to Edmond.
8. Hugs, kisses and laughter will always be the best medicine.
9. Sport is life. As in...there are so many lessons to be taught and learned through sports. It'd be such a waste if they really were...just games.
10. Losing, unfortunately, is a part of life. On the other hand, there is more to life than winning. In the middle of the two...is the process. That, of which, I am learning to appreciate... even more so through my son.

Monica Stephens – "Nuuuuumbeeeeer seeeeveeen."

Kimberly Robins – "Man, Derrick all of this is spot on. Very dope!"

Melissa Costello – "Love this, Derrick! Miss seeing you every day."

Cindy Allen – "So wise, my friend"

THE STORY

My son and I have a deal, I cannot coach him from the sideline. It just doesn't work. I had to stop doing it for three main reasons: 1) I often tell him the opposite of his coach, 2) If I keep telling him what to do, he'll never know what to do, when to do it and how to do it on his own, and 3) It always makes for a terrible and tense ride home. I noticed all three of these things very early, but unfortunately, I pressed through them anyways. I was that dad yelling from the stands trying to get my kid's attention and I didn't stop until he acknowledged what I said. Of course, my intentions were great, but my execution was horrendous. As a result, his passion decreased for the game, our relationship was strained and his skill level slowed for a season.

While looking for ways to connect, I came across this book written by a baseball player. He said one of the things his dad did which he always appreciated was encouraged and supported him. Never coached. Never talked about sports on the way home. Dad never gave tips at the dinner table. Win or lose, no matter what happened, dad always encouraged him by saying, "Man, I love to watch you play."

I'm not saying I don't yell from the sideline often. In fact, I probably do it more than I should, but my son is quick to remind me of our agreement. With all of the humility that I can muster, I admit my error, apologize and say, "Man, I love to watch you play."

THE OBSERVATION

I really do love to watch my son play. I love it when he hustles. Man, he flies like the wind. I love it even more when he's a good sportsman. He wants to make sure he gives the most high-fives out of everyone on his team. I enjoy watching the dots connect and he's able to improve. I love watching when he carries practice over into the game. He's legit in every sense of the word.

I also have to understand he probably loves the game just as much, if not more, than I do. I don't love soccer. Before my son started playing it, I watched it every four years. But I love watching him play soccer. He, on the other hand, actually enjoys the game whether he's playing it or not. He plays it on the video game. He watches it on TV. He wears soccer socks to school. He dribbles while watching soccer vines. This guys loves the sport.

I would also be willing to bet he loves it when his mother, sister and I watch, support and encourage his interest, which happens to be soccer. Whenever he does something great on the field, he looks over to make sure we're watching. Unprovoked, he talks about the game with us on the way home and over dinner. We've learned to allow him to take the lead and not force our interest onto his participation. And no matter what happens during the game, we always let him know how much we enjoy watching him play.

THE LESSON

Encouragement always wins. I can't recall an occasion when encouraging someone has backfired. Now, I'm not suggesting that we encourage people in every area of life. There may be some fundamental things with which we disagree; maybe some areas in which someone is looking for approval and encouragement. That encouragement would be misleading and misplaced. I always think about that when watching singing shows. There is always that one person who gets on stage and performs really badly. I mean, it's obviously to everyone that singing is not their gift nor talent. I think,

"Who would encourage someone to get up there and do that to themselves in front of the entire world?!" (Just my opinion.)

And maybe that is a form of encouragement as well. I know people who don't show potential in a certain area, but they honestly believe this is what they are supposed to be doing. Part of me says, "What kind of friend would I be to let this person do something like this?" The other part of me says, "What kind of friend would I be to not encourage them to pursue their dreams?" Maybe, before that friend got in front of millions of people to sing, their friends did, in fact, tell them it probably wasn't a good idea. At which point, the person who wanted to sing insisted on singing anyway. This caused everyone to switch from criticism to support.

Maybe my son isn't the fastest on the team. Maybe other parents and players are looking at him thinking, "What kind of parent would allow their child to play knowing he has no potential in this sport?" All I know is, my son lights up when he gets on a soccer field. Scratch that. My son lights up putting on the jersey and the cleats. And no matter what happens before or after that, my job is to say, "Man, I love watch you play."

Who are you encouraging? How do you encourage them? Who is encouraging you? How do they encourage you? Do you have those people in your life that encourage you to quit? Do they encourage you to leave your spouse? Maybe they encourage you to cheat on a test or speed down the street or experiment with drugs or stay out past curfew. Maybe you have friends that encourage you to lie or stretch the truth. Maybe they encourage risky behavior. That's not the type of encouragement I'm talking about.

I'm talking about the type of encouragement that pushes you past the moment and into your future and towards becoming your best self. That is the type of encouragement that always wins.

List unique ways in which you encourage people.

_____

_____

_____

_____

_____

_____

_____

_____

_____

_____

_____

_____

_____

_____

LIST 29: PLAYGROUND

(November 7, 2015)

Random questions/statements from my son....

1. "Dad, what's a liquor store?! And why are there so many?!"
2. "I like the way your belly keeps moving after I hit it."
3. "I just had a daymare. Everyone was being chased by large spiders."
4. "Dad, you know what's the best thing I love about pizza?!?! Ranch."
5. "Why do we need money?! Can't we just trade for the things we need?! Kinda like what kids do at lunch."
6. "Dad, you wanna guess how many high-fives I gave away at school today?!"
7. "I'm bored. Never mind. Cause I know you're gonna tell me to go read."
8. "Dad, a kid at school showed me a naked picture of a girl on the school's iPad. And guess what?!?! He did it on purpose. Who does stuff like that?!"
9. "This girl at school told me my skin was too dark to have a girlfriend. I told her, what does my skin have to do with my personality?!?!"
10. **"Sometimes, I find the kid on the playground that no one is playing with... and I play with him."**

Hannah Lee De Ojeda – "#10 is awesome. You guys are doing a great job!"

Sunshine Ponder Cowan – "What an incredible young man you and your bride are raising!"

April Blackwell – "I love reading these. I am sure on a couple of them, you almost choked when he shared it. I am also sure you and your wife are proud of his good choices"

Anibel Sauls – "You are raising an amazing human being."

Marlene Williams – "Aw. Out of the mouth of babes."

Cabrone Brewer – "Haha! 'I like the way your belly keeps moving after I hit it.' You and Tequia have done an outstanding job, sir! You gotta love the things kids say!"

Jerry MrWill Williams – "The best thing I have read in a while"

Monica Stephens – "Its so wonderful that he feels so good about talking to you. Good job, Dad!"

Audrey Stevens – "I miss seeing your kids. Your family is amazing!"

Missy Hoppe – "Love it. He's brilliant just like his dad!"

Mandy Duane – "9 and 10 brought actual tears to my eyes. You guys are doing a great job with those kids!!"

Joshua Pease – "In the feels"

Crystal Williamson – "#9….Wish everyone had that knowledge….and #10…Wish everyone had that type of compassion! You and Tequia are doing an amazing job!"

Sylvia Stevenson – "I just love them. #9 made me want to go find the kid that said that, lol. He's so smart…can you tell him to start working on that trading system?"

Tiffany Willis – "I love this kid. Lol never even met him but he's awesome"

Brittany Clay – "How wise already!"

Heather McFarland – "He sounds absolutely fabulous! Loved his reply to #9. Personality will always trump…(with the good girls anyways) You guys are raising quite a young man!"

Darlene Neal – "That is so adorable!!! And he is obviously very intelligent and you're doing a great job raising him!!! Thanks for sharing!!!"

Yvette White-Martin – "I love this!!"

THE STORY

Hopefully, you aren't tired of reading stories about my kids... because I never tire of telling them. So, here's another.

I can't express the value of seeing my dad do awesome stuff when I was younger. My dad used to drive this big red truck. He also coached four sports. A few times a week, he would drive from block to block, pile kids in the back of Big Red and take them to the park for practice. Depending on the seasons, we would play basketball, baseball, football, swim, wrestle and if we had a little extra time - make pottery, play pool and play ping pong. After practice was over and everyone was done piffling around, he would pile everyone into the back of Big Red again and take them home.

Since my dad coached a lot kids in the neighborhood, everyone was always over to the house. My mom washed clothes for kids who didn't live in our house. She cooked dinners and sent kids away with leftovers. We've had sleepovers and game nights. Our house was the spot. My dad was dad for so many dad-less kids. My mom, the same. When my dad started driving the church van, he would drive around the neighborhood and pick up those same kids and take them to church with our family on Sunday mornings.

Now, that I'm a parent, I allow my children every opportunity to see me do the same things. I take my kids to my mentorship classes. They get to see me facilitate team building sessions. They tag along during volunteer opportunities at elementary schools. They get to be cold during parades. They watch from the window as I push stalled cars out of the street. They see dad babysit children of family friends. We host parties. We got to community events. I wouldn't have it any other way.

As a result of that, one day, my son gets in the car ready to share his highlights of the day. He says, "Dad, I left my friends to go play with someone who was sitting by themselves today. Sometimes, I do that. I find the kid on the playground that no one is playing with...and I play with him. You know why? That's what we [Siers] do."

THE OBSERVATION

Whoever said your children are watching everything you do was telling the absolute truth. They did not under or overshoot with that statement. My children's eyes and ears are glued to our conversation and behavior way deeper than we could ever imagine. I am reminded of this during times like these. He said, "That's what we do." What in the world?! You mean to tell me this little guy has been leaving the comfort of his friends and normal playing routine to tend to complete strangers? That is insane! And even more so, he learned to do that by watching his mother and I?! I can't even put into words how amazing this is.

Let's look at it a slightly different way. Based on our behavior, he decided it is our job as a family to make sure other people are okay. I asked him how does he know this is "what we do"? He mentioned how his mom and I do it all the time. He listed several things we do often and even the rare things we've done he's remembered. Paying for people's groceries. Helping people move. Giving people rides. Dragging other kids along on family day. Hugging and high-fiving our friends. Buying pizzas, driving around town and handing slices out of the window to homeless people. These kids are watchers. These kids are doers. And they are doing what they see us do.

THE LESSON

Knowing my children are watching, not only encourages me in my efforts to do good, but it also makes me overly conscious of the not-so-good things I do. My eating & exercise habits. My use of poorly chosen words. My conversation about people and situations. My thoughts regarding religion, politics or our educational system. How I interact with their mother. The way I communicate with them about body image, work ethic, gender roles and romance. Their acknowledgement of my behavior and conversation shines a bright spot light on my intentions. No longer can I make selfish decisions all willy-nilly. I am held to a higher standard of decision making because, whether I like it or not, I am exampling what healthy, responsible and servant-living looks like.

How long do I have to live this way? At what point are they responsible for living for themselves? What if the way that I live and the example I'm setting doesn't fit the path they choose? I ask these questions often.

I called a pastor friend and asked him, "Where do you and your wife go to dance?" His reply, "We take lessons and dance in a studio." I followed up with, "What if you want to dance outside of the studio?" He said, "We don't." I replied, "Why not?" He said, "It's hard to live in a glass house in a world full of rock throwers."

I'm always looking at people for an example. How did they do it? What are their thoughts? I don't want to re-create the wheel. If someone has found a way which fits my lifestyle, I'll take note, use that as a basis and make adjustments as needed. But because I know I watch people, I know people will be watching me. That said, I'm not sure I will ever completely act from a purely selfish motive. My responsibility toward my neighbor, wife, children, friends, mentees, community is too great to mishandle. I cherish the rapport and relationship I've developed too much to handle it without care.

"But can you spend your entire life living for others? Worrying about what other people think? That will drive you crazy!" (I have a couple of friends who say this often.) I do believe in living life well. It should definitely be lived to the fullest. Some may say, without regret. Anyone who knows me can vouch for my high energy, spontaneous, somewhat risky and entertaining way of living. However, I rarely make those decisions without the greater picture in mind. What's the greater picture? My neighbor, wife, children, friends, mentee and community are the greater picture. Everything must fit within those parameters. Why? Because I know they're watching.

I don't know what life looks like for you. In fact, it's not my job to know what life looks like for you. More specifically, that it's YOUR job to know what life looks like. You decide your boundaries. You decide what the big picture looks like. You know what makes your heart flutter and your eyes light up. You know the expectations you've set for yourself and you are aware of the expectations of others placed on your life. You have a responsibility to at least a few people around you. What are those? Once you have identified all of those things, your life will take shape…and that shape will determine your path and correlating behavior. And the reason it's important is because someone somewhere is on the playground of life…. waiting for you to come play with them. And you'll do it because, that's just what you do.

List some areas in which people rely on you.

LIST 30: LEFTOVER PIZZA

(October 26, 2015)

Random moments....

1. After an assembly at one of the elementary schools, a kindergarten boy gave me a slap on the bottom and said, "Good Job!" Thanks?!
2. As I was walking out of Jimmy's Egg, an older guy pulled up to the front door to let his wife out. As she got out, he leaned over and grabbed her booty. #goals
3. I raced a mini-van in my Explorer on NW Expressway.... and lost. She had to be at least 60. #humbled
4. I saw a lady nurse her baby in church. I was okay with it...
5. I almost ran over a horse in Hinton, OK. A horse....
6. I cried at the new State Farm commercial.... where the parents are dropping their daughter off at college. Dad gets out of the car and takes a picture with his daughter before pulling off. That's gonna be a hard day for me.
7. I had a conversation with my kids about beer and wine this weekend. I think (hope) it went well.
8. A coworker's button came open on her shirt. In my mind, I said, "Hey, your shirt is open." But out loud, I said...."Hey, I can see your boob." Smh....
9. **I fussed at my daughter about a poor choice of clothing she wore. She cried. I felt bad for even**

> **needing to have the conversation. We hugged it out**
> **a few hours later, shared an ice cream and a plate of**
> **left over pizza.**
> 10. My wife is fine. Yup...

Jenn Fitts Higgins – "Lol…I can see your boob!"

Anderson Harrison III – "Man…I always look forward to your randomness!"

Krystal Malveaux – "9. She'll thank you and appreciate the correction later."

Alicia Douglas Rambo – "Lol. The highlight of my day… Derrick's random moments. I see a blog…"

Rachel Jones – "I must say I absolutely love reading your random moments :) thank you for sharing!"

Vickey D. White – "never underestimate a 60 year young person! We got this, been doing it a lot longer! […]"

Michelle Hopper – "My dad once had a horse hit his truck. It damaged his truck more than it was damaged."

Phillis Tyson – "Thanks for your randomness"

Shawna Link – "I can't stop laughing!"

Sanah Bittaye – "You're so entertaining…luv ur Top 10."

T H E   S T O R Y

When it comes to my daughter's clothes, my wife usually runs the show. In fact, if it's at all possible, I try to stay completely out of it. If sackcloth and potato sacks aren't an option, then I don't have an opinion about it. I just trust whatever my wife chooses works like repellant and covers up like a comforter. And you know why? Because I was a 10-year-old boy once. And I'm not sure when or why it happened, but the smell of shampooed hair became more appealing than the sound of squeaky tennis shoes on a gym floor. I started to turn the channel from Thunder Cats to Saved by the Bell just to watch Lark Voorhies prance and smile and prance up and down the halls of Bayside High. Lip gloss lured me in like a moth to a light. Puberty made every straight middle school road crooked and I was there for the ride. SO!....While I can't prevent the little Derricks out there from morphing into raging versions of their adolescent selves, I CAN have some influence on my innocent little princess of a daughter.

Of course, it didn't quite work out the way I planned. In the same way we store up good deeds for the future by investing good deeds into the present. The same law works with mischief. Yep. It works the same way. And I'm not talking about my behavior as a child being reflected in the behavior of the little boys I'm trying to prevent from interacting with my daughter. I'm talking about my daughter being like her father! Strong headed. Independent. Full of her own ideas. Expressive. Risk-taker. Defiant. Creative. Zealous. That said, she wants to dress herself and use her outfit as a canvas of expression.

As life would have it, one day, I was picking my daughter up from school. She comes around the corner in her new fancy pants her and mom picked out for theater and dance rehearsal. I clearly remember mom stating the terms in which these pants could be worn and those terms were clearly being violated as she strutted to the car, smile planted on face and backpack in hand.

She opens the front passenger side door, throws her backpack into the floor, flops into the chair and says, "Hi, Daddy!" I said, "Uhhh...what are you wearing?" She replied, "My fancy new pants! Mom and I picked them out this past weekend. Like em'?!" I replied with a blank stare. She said, "What?!" As I pulled away from the school, I began to firmly explain to her what I thought about those pants. Five minutes passed. 10 minutes passed. 15 minutes passed. After I poured all of my anger and frustration and embarrassment on her pleasant day and her fancy new pants, I noticed alligator tears running down her face. And I immediately felt like CRAP! Not once during that rant did I take her feelings or the scenario into consideration.

I apologized. Detoured from the house. Pulled into an ice cream shop. Requested she break her silence and chime in on the conversation over a double scoop of birthday cake ice cream. We then moved our talk to the house and continued over leftover pizza. We eventually resolved the conversation. I apologized. The new fancy pants have not been an issue since.

THE OBSERVATION

I cannot express how quickly that situation escalated. The moment I saw her, I was blinded by my own fear, frustration, preference, bias and personal experience. I didn't even see a person. I completely looked through my daughter and saw pants. Can you imagine that?! One of the most precious things to me in this world…in the cosmos…I completely disregarded because of a pair of pants. Hopefully, as you read that, you are shaking your head in disbelief because I am shaking my head in disbelief as I write it.

I have run that conversation over and over in my mind at least a hundred times. I've approached it so many different ways. I've taken the compassionate dad approach. "You know, baby girl. I understand you want to be expressive and explorative in your wardrobe, but…". I've taken the fable story-telling dad approach. "You know, princess. I grew up with a young lady that shared your same sense of fashion…..". I've taken the empathetic dad approach. "Gosh, finding clothes that fit our comfort and style can be difficult, huh?". I've taken the "I'll let mom handle this one" approach. "Hey, little momma. When we get home, make sure you talk to mom about wearing those new fancy pants outside of the theater.". However, no matter how many times I run that conversation again, in my mind, heart and spirit, I've taken every other approach than the one I took that day.

THE LESSON

I wonder how many times I've allowed my fear, frustration, bias, preference and personal experience to impact how I interact with someone? The realist in me says, "Of course you allow those things to determine and dictate how you interact with people. You'd be a fool not to! Those are evolutionary protective measures set up to defend against hurt and to decrease the amount of time spent categorizing others for your safety and towards a healthy, productive interaction." The optimist in me says, "Man, I'd hate for someone to do that with me. Especially if those things have a negative impact on our interaction."

My daughter places a lot of value in being able to effectively express her character, personality, mood and vibrance via her outfit. She is also at such an impressionable age that approval to her is hyper-encouraging and disapproval is devasting. And we are working through that...for her to be able to take feedback, whether it be in agreeance with her personal opinion or not....and use it for future reference. As an adult, I am the same way. My livelihood is based on my ability to understand the needs of my clients, successfully address those needs and based on the way I meet those needs, have an impact that hopefully creates change amongst my client's organization and their culture. So, when people agree or disagree with my method; when they approve or disapprove of my approach; when they like or dislike my opinion, it definitely impacts how we interact moving forward. However, more than whether we agree or disagree on the method, approach and opinion, is how we move forward after our stance is established.

After I noticed the pants my daughter was wearing, I had several ways to address the situation. After my client observes and experiences my service via my method, approach and opinion, they have several ways to move forward. Once you observe and form an opinion about someone based on your fear, frustration, bias, preference, personal experience and whatever other filter you are using to size them up, you have several options moving forward. The ability to match the appropriate forward movement with the moment is crucial.

I once heard someone say, "The Golden rule of 'treating someone how you want to be treated' is antiquated. We should now operate on the Platinum rule of 'treating people how THEY want to be treated.' While I'm not completely sold on either, there is some value in both. My daughter is a rock star. She should be treated as such. She is a princess, but everyone won't take the time to see her royalty. It is her right to be free in her expression, but it is my responsibility to teach her how others may interpret her expressiveness.

I'm a rock star facilitator. When I meet with a client and walk into a room full of their people, I bring my A-game every single time. I speak with passion and conviction. I lead every activity with caution and equal abandonment. My voice fills the room with energy. My creativity grows with each encounter. Our rapport builds throughout the day. However, my client also has the right to adjust my facilitation style based on their needs and the goals of the day. If I'm not a good fit, I can adjust or refer them to another facilitator.

Every encounter, whether we agree or disagree, should be salvageable. And most of them, if turned unfruitful and negative, can be mended with ice cream and pizza. Ha! We just have to have the Golden Rule and Platinum Rule available to both sides....and the heart to apply both as needed. Remember, we can't continue to look through the people and only see their pants.

List some ways in which you have applied the Platinum Rule.

_____

_____

_____

_____

_____

_____

_____

_____

_____

_____

_____

_____

_____

_____

_____

WRAP UP

Whoa! You've made it! Thanks for hanging in there with me. Have you ever scrolled through someone's social media feed and felt like you just re-lived those days, weeks and months with them? I know I have. I think thoughts like, "Man, they sure traveled a lot this summer!" OR "Their children have been busy this school year." OR "I'm so glad they sold that house. They've been trying to get rid of it for several months now." Keep in mind, I haven't spoken to that person one time, but I felt like I'm totally caught up on life just by keeping up with their social media.

This bleeds over into our face to face interaction as well. It happens every time. When I see someone I haven't connected with in a while, we often reference each other's social media posts. "Did I see that you and you family just came back from D.C.? How was that?" And they to me, "Ah man, I've been seeing business pick up and the book catching some momentum. How's that going?" I know you've experienced this.

Well, I hope that has happened during this book. I hope you've not only read the words on these pages, but that you've gone back through my social media, scoured the comments and participated in the conversation. If not, maybe you've gone back through your social media and re-read some of the conversations you've had there. At the very least, I hope you begin to see your moments, your days, weeks...your experiences in list form. If you are sitting in a coffee shop, pay attention to the people around you and make a list. Five things you love about your barista. Three things you love about your local coffee shop. Seven type of people you believe are coffee fanatics. Four reasons you MUST have coffee to kick start your day. It works!

Living your life in lists forces you to look longer and to look deeper. Anyone can go to a coffee shop, grab some Joe and head out the door. But how many are willing to maximize the moment by milking it with observation? Who is going to notice the ring tattoo on the finger of the person at the register? Who is going to notice the vintage Nike shoes and slim fitted suit of the dark brew in front of them? Who notices the pay-it-forward and is determined to ask how long it has been going? When we begin to live life like this, every moment becomes a story. Every story becomes a memory. Every memory sticks firm to create a life lived deeply and richly.

CHALLENGE

Start taking advantage of list moments. Heck! Create list moments. You don't know how? I just gave you 30 real-life examples from my personal life. Your life may not look exactly like mine, but that's great because this world doesn't need another Derrick....it would be jacked up...and while everyone would be getting along, nothing would be getting done! Ha! The world needs you! It needs your perspective. It needs your lists. It needs your precious moments in life to be deepened and enriched and unpacked and then shared. Because when you share, you inspire someone else to share.

Start small. What do you like about your workouts? The more reasons you can attach to working out, the more reasons you have to fight against quitting. Why do you like crafting your own beer? 1) I get to control the taste. 2) It takes me mind off of real life stuff. 3) It allows me to have a creative outlet. 4) It plugs me in to a larger community. 5) I love to drink it anyways, so it's a natural interest of mine. COME ON! This is not difficult. It just requires you to shift your focus a little bit. I know you can do it!

Three things I love about tickling my children: it makes them laugh, it increases our physical touch time and it increases our play time together. You could make lists for days! But I'm not asking for days. I'm asking for moments. While you are meditating at the beginning of your day. In the shower. While buying your coffee. Dropping your children off at daycare. Stop and notice. Notice people. Notice the environment. Not the service. Notice the birds and the weather. During the drive in to work. While walking down the hall to your office. While sitting in your fourth meeting of the day. Take notice. During lunch - five things I bet I have in common with people who bring their lunch to work: 1) I bet we are attempting to maximize our time, 2) I bet we are trying to be good with money, 3) I bet we are trying to watch our weight/health, 4) I bet we are trying to leave work early and 5) I bet it's less of a hassle than losing our parking spot, standing in line, only to get back and have to shovel our food in our faces in 10 minutes.

I challenge you. DO IT!

STORY TIME

My follow up to you. Once you become proficient at slowing down and noticing those small moments, begin to flesh out those moments into memories by making them stories. One of the things I've learned from my father is to fall in love with stories. He is such a good story teller. My gosh, I feel like my dad has a story for absolutely everything. And he probably does. It's because he sees life in story form. I swear, he should have been a writer or director in this life.

Develop your moments into memories by making them stories.

I've had so many moments turn into memories because I took the time to appreciate them. Small exchanges while holding a door so someone can walk through...that is a memory made into a story. How?

I was walking into a restaurant wearing my cowboy hat. As I approached the door, I noticed two older ladies walking behind me. I grabbed the door handle, opened the door and stepped to the side to allow them to go in first. As they walked through, one of the said, "I told you he would hold the door." They other said, "The cowboy hat was a dead giveaway. I've never met a rude man in a cowboy hat." That is a moment I will never forget. Why? Because in my mind, I've chewed on it several different ways. By doing something I would have normally done anyways, I am now a part of their conversation... a part of their life...a part of their memories. Had I not been wearing the hat, would they have thought otherwise about me holding the door? Was it my age? My race? The distance of me to the door compared to where they were? I don't know, but they made my day...and made one of my stories. I bet I made one of their stories as well.

Lists lead to memories. And when we spend this much time living with and learning from life, it rewards us richly.

MY LIFE OF LISTS
PART 2

I initially started to pack this book with 60 posts instead of 30, but thought that may be a little too long. If you made it to this part of the book and spent time with each story, it's deeper observation and the lessons I learned from each one, I'm sure you've got the gist by now. However, you're going to need a refresher in a while. A booster shot of sorts. Everyone always does. Some people go back and read the same book several times. Feel free to do that with this one as well. However, sometimes people need fresh material that echoes the same voice and repaints the same picture with fresh paint. My hope is that *My Life of List, Volume 2* will be that echo and fresh paint for your journey of creating lists, making them memories and sharing those stories.

COMMENTS INDEX

PUT ON SOCKS
(April 15, 2016)

Jason Zielke – "Just keep it in a little perspective....It was one and half classes this week. Next week shoot for 2?"

Jeremey Fultz – "I haven't been able to do that since age 28."

Jonathan Tatum – "bro you are too funny [...]"

CHEW ON IT
(April 14, 2016)

Jason Zielke – "Number 7 happens daily...That's why I gather all the laundry and put it in the washer before I go to tribe. Not picking up the floor after. Today I had trouble washing my hair...."

Amanda Williams-Siebert – "You did not pick it up. Lolololo! I started back today. It's rough but so worth it."

BEAUTIFUL MEMORIES
(April 10, 2016)

Tiffany Whisman – "I like that reminder, even with adults."

Brendon Williams – "These reflections are great"

Rachael Fugate – "I always thought someone needs to write a book about the things learned from 'soccer life'. There are so many valuable lessons learned ON the field and ON the sidelines."

Walela Knight – "#8 so much! I have such amazing wonderful friends who also love Trent."

LOVE-HANDLES
(April 8, 2016)

Sybil Burrell – "Reading these comments I think I'm a pretty cool mom for keeping my comments to myself! Lol #9"

Jaime Taylor – "10. (Derrick to self) Where's that amazing counselor at with my hug?

:-) By the way, your son was outstanding today in that play!"

LEND A HAND
(April 7, 2016)

Missy Hoppe – "YES!!! SO MANY HEARTS!!"

Tiffany Whisman – "8 and 9. Well and all of the rest too."

Robin Summers Gonzalez – "You. Just YOU Derrick Sier!!! You are awesome!"

MY NEIGHBOR ASKED
(April 6, 2016)

Jennifer Bridges – "These. Never. Get. Old. Ever!"

Jerry MrWill Williams – "Wonderfully random as always"

Jaime Taylor – "[…] #7. That's not allowed to happen. I like hugging you too much. Oh, and these posts are always awesome (there an affirmation, just in case)."

Rachel Clapp – How lucky are we to know you? #blessed #youisawesome :-)"

Barry Bergstrom – "It was a bad call. You weren't the only good parent yelling. You're an amazing man and I'm thankful to have you in my life."

HIGHS AND LOWS
(March 23, 2016)

Missy Hoppe – "I had a 'Derrick' moment today!! I thought of you!

Joshua Pease – "I am gonna start recording my 'Derrick' moments"

Amy Parker – "Full frontal hugs are not just appropriate, they are needed!"

Billie Smith – "A friend of my daughter's recently said, 'you guys ask a lot of questions.' Man, we don't know how to skim the surface. These lists make my day"

EAR HAIR
(March 21, 2016)

Jenn Fitts Higgins – "I just heart you, friend!!"

Marika Chambers – "I am cracking up!!!"

Carmon Williams – "I really really want u to know these posts make me smile on m tough days lol #3! #8 happened to me! I laughed so hard reading this!"

COOL PEOPLE
(March 16, 2016)

Brie A. Reynolds – "Derrick Sier is a great man! A true inspiration of manhood and authenticity."

Amanda Williams-Siebert – "#1. You're so awesome."

Melissa Jones Chunu – "You're awesome!!!! Great inspiration!!!!!!"

Ashley Neely – "You rock!"

Bryant Andrews Jr. – "You at Walmart too much lol"

Joshua Pease – "This, I need to strive to be like this."

Missy Hoppe – "I want to follow you around one of these days. I love you stories!"

WHAT YALL DOING IN HERE?
(March 8, 2016)

Jessica Nilsen – "I love your posts! They brighten my day!!! Parenting is detective work for sure!"

Kelda S. Slater – "Yaaasss! I think I've said all of these to the seven year old!"

Monica Stephens – "Thank God!!! It's not just my kids! LOL"

Phillis Tyson – "Love it. You have to be quick on your feet with children…so I've heard"

Cessnie Shelton – "Derrick Sier you are so CRAZY! But sir you must be a fly on the wall in my house. Too Funny!"

Judie Lavender – "LOL cause they make us do that LOL"

HOLDING HANDS
(February 26, 2016)

James Powell III – "I gotta start hanging out with you!!!!"

Cassi Mitzs – "#4 I actually laughed out loud"

Katrina McCaslin – "HOW do you catch all these things!!!"

Kristi Clingenpeel Maxwell – "You've had an interesting week my friend!!!! #4 is the best!!!"

Jeannie McMahan – "Dude, there is nothing you won't write about, and the morning people won't DO?! Hahaha"

E.J. Johnson – "smh, we are an entertaining species"

Rebecca Simcoe – "You make my day! Thank you."

Joshua Pease – "These are the best updates!"

Donny Chastain – "I wanna hang out half a day with you and take notes. We will prolly laugh the whole time. Especially on the golf course. Now that's funny stuff there. […]"

Mandy Mayberry – "I think my life would be more fun if I rode with you!"

LAUGHING
(February 20, 2016)

Shaunteia Powell – "I am so happy you came and played with us!!!!"

Johnathan Powell – "It was an awesome time. We will be doing a lot more of this soon."

Tiffany Whisman – "I saw the same."

Ashley Semone – "Jeez Derrick that was beautiful! Makes me excited for spring!"

FREESTYLE
(February 11, 2016)

Reggie Pratcher – "Voicemail because your Voice smalls freestyle is a classic."

Lashonda Malrey-Horne – "So sweet! Glad you know how lucky you are. I expect something like 'stays fine for me.' Lol"

Jyntel L. Tipton – "I love this Sier!!!!"

Christi Perrin – "Saaawweeeet way to start the Valentine's Day weekend DUDE!! BOOM! ;-) On the serious note however… isn't your WIFE GRAND! Amen and amen!! Blessings to you and yours Sir!"

Lindsay Hale Parke – "This is a great idea. I love the appreciation of your spouse."

LaTonya Harrison Porter – "Award Winning post!!"

Sybil Burrell – "We need more Derrick Sier's of the world. It sure would be a better place."

Gina Michelle Henson Marshall – "What a great compliment!! Well said."

Jessica Wagner – "D, so very sweet! She's amazing and it's nice to see a man celebrate his wife! ~j"

DeAnna J. Ogola – "Sounds like a Proverbs 31st woman!"

SNUGGLE TIME
(January 29, 2016)

NONE

FOCUS
(January 22, 2016)

Chrisinda Gonzalez – "Derrick, you are incredible!!!! Just wanted you to know."

Tequia Sier – "Dad to many…starting with mine. Thanks!"

Heather McFarland – "You're all sorts of amazingness!"

THE EXTRA MILE
(January 21, 2016)

Chris Cole Williams – "Good stuff brother!!!"

Heather McFarland – "Love this post! These points are SPOT ON!"

Bill Moyers – "if all couples did things like this for each other there would be far less divorce"

Robin Summers Gonzalez – "Amen brother. AMEN!!"

Brie A. Reynolds – "'Going the extra mile sometimes is only a few feet.' Love this!"

Kristin Jacoway Fitzgerald – "I kind of consider you my FB Life Coach. Our first point is SPOT ON & something I needed to hear today."

Paul Geisinger – "Couldn't have said it better myself! Great words brother!!

HUG MORE OFTEN
(January 18, 2016)

Latoya Monique – "its okay you never know til you try... LOL...next year at the end go up to the school bands and hug them im sure you get the last 22"

Terri L Dobyns-Brockman – "You are such an inspiration Derrick!"

BOOTYQUAKES
(January 6, 2016)

Nailah J. Pennington – "LOL My kids found this hilarious"

Joshua Pease – "Canadian Hello is new!"

Mark Johnson – "What a gas!"

Monica Stephens – "So now we know where they get their sense of humor!"

Ceanti' Aldridge – "Dookie dust??!!!!! Haaaaa!!!!"

LaToya L. Davis-Mason – "I could hang with your kids"

Ashley Rhodes – "Dookie dust has my side hurting from laughing!!!!!!!!!!"

Nikki Young – "BHAHAHAHAHAHA! "Dookie Dust" tho?!?! Yeah, those are DEFINITELY your kids!!!!"

ERRANDS
(December 16, 2015)

Jarred Pettijohn – "Here's one that annoys me the most. 'I could care less.' – This means that you care. If you didn't care, you 'couldn't care less' which is the correct way to say what you are intended to say."

Jeannie McMahan – "Ha. When I was a little girl I loved using the word 'actually'. I read once that people who say 'actually' may be lying. Actually, I don't care, because I like the word…"

Danni Dizzy – "You are ridiculous bro!!"

MaryBeth Omido – "Mmm, can I add to your comment about Actually--it can turn a compliment into an insult in an instant. 'You look good today.' vs 'You actually look good today.'"

Katy Janaye – Not that you asked, but words that annoy me are LITERALLY, when it's NOT literal compared to something figuratively. And anything EVER. Let's be honest, no one was around for the entire time of the whole universe so no one knows if it was the best, coolest, worst, etc., EVER."

Jennifer Thomas – "I'm surprised irregardless is not on the list because it is at the top of mine."

Andrew Hamm – "Bruh. Truth. And I feel convicted."

Pam Dehorney – "'Honestly' is the word for me. It implies that everything that was said previously to using the word 'honestly' was dishonest."

Cara McKenzie Fain Hardee – "I just laughed out loud."

HOLDING HANDS WITH A STRANGER
(December 9, 2015)

Billie Smith – "I am LOL at #9. I'm a touchy feely, even with strangers, so I'm guilty of picking lint off someone's shoulder. This whole list made me laugh!"

Andria Campbell – "Beautiful!"

Leah Shannon – "Stranger danger!"

Alan K. Swan – "busted."

Godlove Ngo – "Just another day in the life of Derrick."

Tequia Sier – "#7 please stay safe…and ALIVE. I need you!!! #3/4 – People always fall in love w/you no matter how outrageous you get. Stop encouraging him people! ;)"

Kimberly Pruitt-Zachery – "You Rock!!!"

Jerry MrWill Williams – "You are so random…Lmao"

Jason Zielke – "I stopped a bearded hipster and told him his fly was down."

Gina Michelle Henson Marshall – "You take 'Love thy neighbor' to a whole 'nother' level!!! Good job!"

WHAT'S IN YOUR HAND?
(December 4, 2015)

Jawan Johnson – "Wise lessons sir."

Chris Peacock – Beautiful job though bro bro…where people are complaining about this generation, ESPECIALY black young men…it is rare that people actually step up and attempt to make a change in someone's life…but people are quick to complain. Be the change you want to see. It only takes ONE… and usually STARTS with one!!!"

HARD TO TAKE
(December 2, 2015)

Kimberly Pruitt-Zachery – "#1 I can't help with cutting the tree but I can bring over one of the patty pies and some coffee."

Sunshine Ponder Cowan – "We loved seeing you – but the visit was too short."

Robin Summers Gonzalez – "#4 though! Best way to be, my friend!"

Briana Steelman – "My favorite post always in my news feed! Don't stop!"

Alicia Douglas Rambo – "No chainsaw here, but I do have two arms and two legs that are pretty good at hauling and stacking the branches after they've been cut…"

Marcellus Coleman – "#2 – is it wrong if I'm mad and impressed by her at the same time??"

1 2 - 0
(November 28, 2015)

Brad Davis – "You have 10 down so add 91 more and your book is complete."

Mark Johnson – "A book? You've only got 91 more to go…."

Hannah Lee De Ojeda – "I've got one for your book! Winning as a team is more fun than winning by yourself. Reb got third in both her swimming relay and the individual backstroke event. She was so much more excited about placing in the relay even though the relay was 3rd out of 5 teams and backstroke was 3rd out of 15 swimmers. Kids don't evaluate it like that though. It's just fun to win with your friends. :)"

Gregory Coleman – "[…] I'm always more interested in my son learning to coach the game than playing. More opportunities when his playing days are over. #DreamCoach

#LifeCoach #SportsCoach #BusinessCoach

Leon Fowler – "Oh man I could help you write that book!! Worst thing to do is not show up for games. OR missing most of the games and promising them you will be there at the next one and just not show up."

Sonia Cavazoz – "Luv this!!!! Having 2 boys in sports can be very nerve wrecking. I literally read a book on Football & Basketball so I could understand better & let me tell you… years later I have the most INTENSE convos w my sons! […] A coach/athlete is the GREATEST thing because they so LISTEN! Trust me! Great job, Derrick!"

Marcellus Coleman – "I've observed No. 7 from the perspective of the losing team. It's so discouraging for children to see the winning tea, get affirmed by their parents; while they themselves see the following responses: 1 – wow the coach sucked 2 – they should have played my kid 3 – you didn't do good enough 4 – better luck next time."

Rachael Fugate – "13 years and counting being a sports parent. […] You learn a lot about yourself! The good and bad. The one thing I know I did right was always be there."

Sara Carreno – "Sports were my life as a kid. As a parent I'm already burnt out. The drama and race to the top is too much!"

KIDS SLEEP
(November 23, 2015)

Prince Wong – "I love your gear hug, brother, I know it sounds awkward, but you make all the troubles melt away when you give me that smile with your arms wide open. Thank you for making possible change in all our lives."

Alex Mott – "That's a good list bro."

Briana Steelman – "I'm so glad we're friends!"

Phillis Tyson – "I love your positive postings they make me smile"

Kristi Clingenpeel Maxwell – "You are the best hugger!!!!!"

YOU'RE THE GUY
(November 18, 2015)

Drea AP – "You are one of THE most awesome souls I have ever had the fortune of meeting!! Thank you for these types of posts!"

Victor Viney – "Yes…"

Billie Smith – "I LOVE these posts because I relate to everyone last one of them! Mom to a teenager, girl even, AND working with the similar student situations on the daily. I cried just last week when an 8th grade girl talked about her mom saying in bed for days, depressed and drinking. How do you shake something like that off? You don't. You apply it when struggling with #10. Have a fabulous day!"

Mel Gaines Smith – "These posts of yours always make my day!!!!"

Jaime Taylor – "#4: gotta love the 3rd grade retention law! You're so funny--I look forward to these posts. And your wife IS precious!!"

Shayne Peffer – "You're my favorite!! I miss you!!"

Nicki French – "I would buy your book :-)"

Marcellus Coleman – "I love this. Thank you for posting this. Makes my day."

Lashonda Malrey-Horne – "As usual another great post. And your daughter is right, you can't talk about girl stuff. […] You can't say anything. Her momma will take care of it!"

Mitzi Dawn Smith – "Keep em coming! Love these updates."

Heather McFarland – "I ALWAYS enjoy reading these! Your perspective and soul is one of a kind!"

Cara McKenzie Fain Hardee – "SNICK. ERS. ICE. CREAM. SNICK. ERS. ICE, CREAM. SNICKERS ICE CREAM."

Jessica Lauren – "This is great. Hope you are well Derrick – sounds like you are!!"

Laura Ragon – "I hope you are saving these to publish for a book one day soon."

Sarah Odusi – "Start a book of your random moments."

Jo Garcia – "I love the bonus!"

Michelle Cullen – "Always choose serving people/ That's a no brainer. Trust me there will come a day and you reflect back and will be glad you choose people over chasing money."

Chris Snoddy – "Love it!"

Mark Johnson – "Keep em' coming!"

LOVE
(November 14, 2015)

Judie Lavender – "Love it."

Tiffany Whisman – "I mean wow. Love."

Kimberly Pruitt-Zachery – "Gotta love it!!!"

Jennifer Bridges – "I love your posts!!!!"

Marya Byers – "I love you Derrick Sier and this is why! U are an amazing person!"

Heather Strong – "We love you back."

Robin Summers Gonzalez – "Exactly how I feel my friend. I don't judge people. I don't presume to do my Savior's job. Love you to pieces"

Mandy Duane – "Blessed to know you!!"

Brad Brown – "Sounds like a man with a platform! Love = truth. Truth = Gospel. Gospel = Love. Sometimes love doesn't = P.C."

MENTORSHIP
(November 12, 2015)

Katie Dow – "I always look forward to your posts!"

Sandy Goins-Pratcher – "Bonus! #mwif"

Cabrone Brewer – "Your high-top was on point back then though!"

Lindsey Jones – "Your weeks are super entertaining! #lifewithDerrickSier I think it should be a TV show"

Jessica Nilsen – "I too look forward to your posts! I'm a hugger too! Keep doing what you're doing!"

Jazman Nicole – "Huggers rule the world!"

Moheb Mark Atia – "Too bad that it's you that has to 'learn'. Keep smilin' that'll disarm the grumpy"

Julie Wade Crum – "#8 Kids keep us humble. Love your posts, Derrick Sier. I always read them to Andy so he can enjoy them too."

Rebecca Tyler – "Number 10 is sooooo me! The power of a great hug is magnificent!"

Jaime Taylor – "I love your hugs! And in my job, it's pretty much given that I will always need one!"

Noble Sandlin – "I'm a hugger too, Derrick Sier. It's the way I was raised!"

Sean Johnson – "#2 made me holler in the doctor's office….. Lol"

Mandy Duane – "These make my day. You should write a book."

Tamia Taylor – "I love you."

Shanon C. Norton – "Love these! It's awesome how observant u are!"

ENCOURAGEMENT ALWAYS WINS
(November 8, 2015)

Monica Stephens – "Nuuuuumbeeeeer seeeeveeen."

Kimberly Robins – "Man, Derrick all of this is spot on. Very dope!"

Melissa Costello – "Love this, Derrick! Miss seeing you every day."

Cindy Allen – "So wise, my friend"

PLAYGROUND
(November 7, 2015)

Hannah Lee De Ojeda – "#10 is awesome. You guys are doing a great job!"

Sunshine Ponder Cowan – "What an incredible young man you and your bride are raising!"

April Blackwell – "I love reading these. I am sure on a couple of them, you almost choked when he shared it. I am also sure you and your wife are proud of his good choices"

Anibel Sauls – "You are raising an amazing human being."

Marlene Williams – "Aw. Out of the mouth of babes."

Cabrone Brewer – "Haha! 'I like the way your belly keeps moving after I hit it.' You and Tequia have done an outstanding job, sir! You gotta love the things kids say!"

Jerry MrWill Williams – "The best thing I have read in a while"

Monica Stephens – "Its so wonderful that he feels so good about talking to you. Good job, Dad!"

Audrey Stevens – "I miss seeing your kids. Your family is amazing!"

Missy Hoppe – "Love it. He's brilliant just like his dad!"

Mandy Duane – "9 and 10 brought actual tears to my eyes. You guys are doing a great job with those kids!!"

Joshua Pease – "In the feels"

Crystal Williamson – "#9....Wish everyone had that knowledge....and #10...Wish everyone had that type of compassion! You and Tequia are doing an amazing job!"

Sylvia Stevenson – "I just love them. #9 made me want to go find the kid that said that, lol. He's so smart...can you tell him to start working on that trading system?"

Tiffany Willis – "I love this kid. Lol never even met him but he's awesome"

DeAnna J. Ogola – "Yall are raising a true Gem! How old is he? Arranged marriage? I have a daughter!!"

Brittany Clay – "How wise already!"

Heather McFarland – "He sounds absolutely fabulous! Loved his reply to #9. Personality will always trump...(with the good girls anyways) You guys are raising quite a young man!"

Darlene Neal – "That is so adorable!!! And he is obviously very intelligent and you're doing a great job raising him!!! Thanks for sharing!!!"

Yvette White-Martin – "I love this!!"

LEFTOVER PIZZA

(October 26, 2015)

Jenn Fitts Higgins – "Lol…I can see your boob!"

Anderson Harrison III – "Man…I always look forward to your randomness!"

Krystal Malveaux – "9. She'll thank you and appreciate the correction later."

Alicia Douglas Rambo – "Lol. The highlight of my day… Derrick's random moments. I see a blog…"

Rachel Jones – "I must say I absolutely love reading your random moments :) thank you for sharing!"

Vickey D. White – "never underestimate a 60 year young person! We got this, been doing it a lot longer! […]"

Michelle Hopper – "My dad once had a horse hit his truck. It damaged his truck more than it was damaged."

Phillis Tyson – "Thanks for your randomness"

Shawna Link – "I can't stop laughing!"

Sanah Bittaye – "You r so entertaining…luv ur Top 10."

CREATE YOUR OWN LIST ABOUT THIS BOOK!

On this page, I want you to create a list of ten things you enjoyed about this book. THEN, 1) follow me on social, if you don't already 2) take a picture of yourself with the book and 3) post your list from this page and a picture with you and the book.

_____

_____

_____

_____

_____

_____

_____

_____

_____

_____

I love connecting with people, old friends and new friends. I believe this will be a great way for you and I to do so!

FOLLOW ME
ON SOCIAL MEDIA

OMOS_Sier

Derrick Sier

Sier55

OMOS Team Building

Sier55